KID THINK

Revolutionary New Insights Into Dealing With the Six Most Common Behavioral Problems of Children

DR. WM. LEE CARTER

WORD PUBLISHING
Dallas · London · Vancouver · Melbourne

Library of Congress Cataloging-in-Publication Data

Carter, Wm. Lee.
    KidThink : revolutionary new insights into dealing with the six most common behavioral problems of children / William Lee Carter
      p. cm.
    ISBN 0–9452–7633–8 (hc)
      0–8499–3565–2 (tp)
    1. Emotional problems of children. 2. Child rearing—religious aspects—Christianity. I. Title. II. Title : KidThink
BF723.E6C36   1994
649'.64—dc20

                                      93–44761
                                         CIP

Printed in the United States of America.

4 5 6 9 LB 10 9 8 7 6 5 4 3 2 1

Contents

Foreword

In an exasperated tone, parents often ask me questions like:

"Why does Johnny act that way?"

"I've done everything I know to do, but I can't control her. Where do I turn now?"

"He can't seem to get along with anybody! He is driving me crazy! Can you help?"

"I don't know what's wrong . . . . She's a sweet girl, but she's so quiet. She won't talk to me. What's going on inside her?"

Being a parent is the most difficult job in the world! Changes in children's ages, friends, desires, and situations (and changes in us, too) challenge our capacity to understand our children's needs. At some point, virtually all parents feel confused and discouraged.

In this insightful book, Lee Carter helps us understand why our children act like they do. He helps us understand how they think and how their behavior is a reflection of their thought processes. He shows how each kind of child is different and how parents can respond properly to their unique needs. The case studies, practical suggestions, clear explanations, and biblical perspectives give this book both warmth and punch.

Understanding our children is a major part of good parenting. Then, and only then, can we make good choices about the specifics of:

- how much "help" we need to give them;
- how much control is needed at each age;
- how we can let them learn to fail and not be devastated;
- how we can affirm without smothering;
- how we can help them grow into loving, responsible adults.

Without this understanding, we may be able to control our children's behavior for a while, but we—and our children—will reap a bitter and painful harvest in their late adolescence and early adulthood. Lee's insights give us the "handles" we need so that we can lovingly and responsibly influence our children.

Parents need to talk about their children. The questions in this book provide excellent small group content for couples and single parents. Interaction with other parents will give you added perception and stimulate your creativity as you look for answers. A group can also provide the support and encouragement you need when you feel confused, hopeless, hurt, and angry because of your relationship with your children.

Probably the most significant feature of Lee's writing is that he offers hope. Confused and discouraged parents need a lot of that! I trust you—and your children—will benefit greatly from *KidThink*.

ROBERT S. McGEE

RAPHA, INC.   PRESIDENT AND FOUNDER

Preface

As I COUNSEL CHILDREN and adolescents, I frequently share my viewpoint of how the optimum family should function. Even the most argumentative and ill–behaved child will agree that parents are to be in charge of the family. That fact seems to be a given characteristic of the family unit. When I explain to the young person that I will be approaching his family with the belief that the most effective parents are those who are able to see the world through a child's eyes, I invariably receive a positive reaction.

Children who feel understood by their parents without fail feel a greater sense of respect. Their willingness to cooperate with parents will rise. Similarly, the parent who learns to view life as does his child finds it easier to be objective about the response he must give to the developing personality. I like to tell parents that their knowledge of their child's emotional and behavioral tendencies coupled with the wisdom they have accrued through their life experiences can result in effective family leadership and productive decision–making.

I find that I learn the greatest lessons about family life by observing and studying families in action. I will try to bring alive some of the typical dilemmas, exchanges, and behaviors seen in the patterns discussed in this book. Be patient with me as I explain the selected behaviors and why they might occur in a child. I have chosen to wait until the end of each chapter to offer solutions to the problems laid out in that chapter. I promise not to leave you hanging in your quest to know what to do or say in response to your child's behavior.

I believe one of the greatest challenges God gives us is to develop a full understanding of our own emotional makeup and that of our children. The Scriptures are full of wisdom that can be applied to our relationships with others, especially those with whom we are most closely attached—our family members. Not only will I speak to the emotional and behavioral needs of the child, but I will also weave into the reading material my strong belief that we cannot be fully effective as parents unless we also recognize that our spiritual heritage offers us a wisdom that can propel us toward our goal of personal and family fulfillment.

I am indebted to many individuals for their help and support in the writing of this book. Not the least of these individuals are my wife, Julie, and my three daughters Emily, Sarah, and Mary. Through the interactions we have had as a family, I am continually thankful for the lessons I have learned about life and family dynamics. There is little doubt that the knowledge I have gleaned from these four people has surpassed the accumulated years of education I received in order to be qualified to be a counselor to others.

It is my sincere hope that your study of the concepts presented in the pages to follow will enrich your interactions with your children as you guide them through their formative years of youth.

My philosophy of life is rooted in the Judeo–Christian tradition, and I have found that the Scriptures are full of wisdom. Throughout this book, I will refer to passages from the Bible as resources of insight and direction for ourselves and our family relationships. If you do not consider yourself to be a Christian, please do not discount this valuable resource.

WM. LEE CARTER, ED.D.

Introduction—
Job Description of a Parent

SITTING IN MY OFFICE WERE Mr. and Mrs. Mason, discussing with me the progress their family had made after several weeks of family counseling. The Masons had come to learn more effective management and communication techniques in an effort to properly raise their two young sons. Both parents were struck by the contrasting differences between the behavior styles of their boys.

Mrs. Mason remarked, "When I first became a parent, I naively thought that if I showed enough love and attention to my children, everything would turn out just fine for our family. I had little forewarning that the individual personalities of my sons would be so different. The discipline techniques that work with one may be totally ineffective with the other. I feel that I've had to become an expert on my boys' personality traits so that I can anticipate the needs of each child and react in the most appropriate way."

Being a parent is hard work! There is little doubt that your children can simultaneously provide a sense of pride and accomplishment and an exasperating feeling of defeat.

I have chosen to concentrate on six of the most common emotional and behavioral conditions of children and adolescents that bewilder parents. A separate chapter is devoted to each of these behavioral types, but be aware that a child may certainly display more than one set of characteristics. Children are quite complex in their behavior and may act completely different on one day as compared to another. Yet, I find that children make sense once we can understand their emotional makeup and learn how they respond to the world around them.

Each of the following chapters contains essentially the same outline. The child's behavioral tendency is described and then analyzed for factors that might develop into a negative pattern. Guidelines for handling the given behavior are then offered. The parent's understanding of the child's personality style is important in effective management of his or her behavior. I operate under the assumption that children act as they do for a reason. A thorough understanding of the child's point of view allows the adult to respond to the child's specific needs.

One of Jesus' summary statements in the Sermon on the Mount exhorts us to "be perfect, therefore, as your Heavenly Father is perfect" (Matt. 5:48). Most commentators accept this word of encouragement as a challenge to be all we are capable of being. As parents we can maximize our potential influence over developing children by willingly studying the world as seen from their eyes. Such an understanding greatly enhances our effectiveness.

Before we get to each chapter's guidelines for specific patterns of behavior, we need to begin with several common denominators that apply to all families. Applying the following broad rules for behavior management and adding the more specific recommendations suggested in each of the following chapters should provide an effective approach to family management.

The parent is the leader of the family.

An important task in family counseling is to study the communication and behavior patterns of family members. Such an analysis often reveals that a child is the one running the household. While the age levels and the personality styles of the children may influence a family's activities to a large degree, it must be the parents who bear the responsibility for the general atmosphere that is present in the home.

We are rightly taught that all family members are of equal value to God and should regard one another with a respect that acknowledges the God–given worth of every human life. Yet because of the age, experience, and wisdom of the adults, the parents have leadership responsibilities in the home. A democratic process is fine for certain family policies and decisions. It is the parents, though, who are jointly and equally responsible for the role of *leadership* within the family. A disruption in family structure occurs when children take charge of the home atmosphere.

Several ways in which a child or adolescent may inappropriately assume the leadership role of the family include:

- Playing on the emotions of the parents to influence decisions.

- Refusing to cooperate as retaliation for parental discipline.

- Use of intimidation or threats to avoid disciplinary action.

- Acting helpless as a way of evoking parental guilt.

- Blaming others in order to shift responsibility.

- Purposely breaking rules to test established limits.

- Claiming ignorance as an excuse for poor judgment.

The list could continue, but the point here is that the inexperience of childhood requires adult supervision and guidance. The parent who refrains from allowing a child to take control of the home environment will eventually experience a much greater sense of satisfaction in observing the maturity of that child.

Maturity is a lifelong process. As a child gathers experience in this process, parental direction is needed to minimize the mistakes that inevitably will be made. With age, parental influence lessens as the child's independence increases. The effective parent exhibits leadership by:

- Displaying emotional control when faced with conflict.

- Making decisions in a confident manner.

- Soliciting the viewpoint of other family members.
- Allowing for differences of opinion.
- Offering abundant compliments and rewards.
- Admitting to mistakes that have been made.
- Sharing responsibilities according to individual capabilities.
- Managing time in an organized manner.

Some understand that they are to lead their children, but they lack confidence in their leadership qualities. An examination of biblical characters reveals a wide assortment of individuals, shortcomings notwithstanding, who found themselves in leadership positions. Peter with his bad temper, Moses with his speaking handicap, and mild–mannered Mary are but a few examples of people who were given heavy responsibilities and yet successfully influenced others positively.

It is a given fact that all families encounter various trials and traumas. The inclination of the child will be to react to these circumstances with his limited knowledge and understanding of life. It is the parent who must display the leadership that draws upon the experiences of his advanced years. Any child who takes control of the home environment will encounter unnecessary emotional harm as an inevitable byproduct of his own lack of wisdom and judgment.

—Case Study—

Teresa was almost 16 years old and could not wait for her birthday to arrive. She had been promised by her parents that once she reached that age, she would be granted increased social freedom.

The first Friday night following her birthday, Teresa made plans to go out with some friends for a celebration. Before she left the house, her father told her, "Teresa, I want you to be home no later than 11:00 o' clock."

"Eleven o'clock! Why can't I come in later? You told me that once I turned 16 I could stay out later. I have already told my friends I could probably stay out until midnight. I can't come in at eleven o'clock!" Teresa pleaded her case, but to no avail.

Dad was firm when he responded. "Eleven o'clock is late enough. We'll see about moving the time back later if you show responsibility."

Teresa was in a state of disbelief over her father's rule. She felt betrayed. "Dad, you don't understand. My friends are expecting me to stay out later with them. I can't disappoint them. Don't you understand?"

"Oh, I fully understand, but I want you home at eleven o'clock."

By now Teresa was mad. "You can't understand! If you did, you would let me stay out later. I hate it when you say you understand me, because you don't!"

The world should be viewed through the child's eyes.

There are few parents who have escaped similar accusations by their children. Children and teenagers tend to equate understanding with agreement. A young person will typically think that a parent displays understanding only if he lets the child have his own way.

I am of the belief that because the parent is the leader of the home, he must have a full comprehension of his child's emotional makeup and behavioral tendencies. Such knowledge allows the parent to make decisions that are in the child's best interests. But understanding the child does not mean agreeing with the child in every situation. The parent's advanced wisdom will at times lead to decisions that are unpopular with the child.

A primary task of parenthood is to communicate to the child that he is indeed understood. The parent's words and actions must assure the child that life has been viewed from his youthful reference point. Then any inevitable unpopular decisions the parent must make will be more readily accepted. Guidelines for developing and communicating greater understanding of the child are as follows:

- Focus on both the verbal and nonverbal messages of the child.

- Make an attempt to "read between the lines" of your child's statements.

- Respond to your child in such a way that it is clear that you heard what he said and understood the emotion with which it was stated.

- Refrain from language or dialogue that puts a distance between you and the child. Don't allow the child to engage you in unnecessary arguments.

- Talk in terms the child can understand.

- Demonstrate flexibility if the situation allows for it.

- Avoid making predictions, accusations, or judgments that the child will most likely reject.

- Offer your full attention when the child is speaking to you.

When the parent develops an understanding of his child, he can adapt to the individual needs of that child. Flexibility can be shown when called for. The need for discipline can be determined. Respect will be communicated. Cooperation will be encouraged, for a child who feels understood will be more accepting of the parents' role of leadership.

The parent's self-concept is reflected in the child.

As the parent establishes the atmosphere of the home environment, perhaps the most important element he brings is his own concept of himself. The self-concept of the parent in many ways determines his response to the child. Note the different atmosphere in the home led by parents with a healthy self-concept as opposed to the home led by parents with an unhealthy self-image.

Healthy Self–Concept	*Unhealthy Self–Concept*
Balances personal and family activities.	Becomes wrapped up in the child's world.
Displays dependability toward the child.	Fails to follow through with promises.
Asserts emotions in a controlled fashion.	Has poor control over anger.
Maintains an objective outlook.	Worries continually about the outlook of the child.

cont'd

Healthy Self–Concept	**Unhealthy Self–Concept**
Acknowledges the child's right to his emotions.	Ignores the child's feelings.
Shows poise in reacting to problems.	Overreacts to problem situations.
Displays confidence in decisions that have been made.	Shows indecision in decision–making.
Provides abundant encouragement to the child.	Routinely finds fault with the child.
Views life optimistically.	Expects the worst to happen.
Displays flexibility in behavior management.	Follows rules with rigidity.
Allows choices within reasonable guidelines.	Makes too many decisions for the child.
Makes family activity part of the daily schedule.	Spends too much time pursuing personal interests.
Communicates openly and and honestly.	Fails to disclose genuine thoughts feelings.
Shows sincerity and warmth toward others.	Keeps emotions safely hidden from others.
Sees life from the child's viewpoint.	Looks at life in a one–dimensional fashion.

There is not a simple formula that allows a child to enter adulthood with a healthy self–image. Many adults can recount a series of harmful relationships or circumstances that contributed to their own negative view of themselves. Others are able to re-direct a harmful past and during adulthood find renewal and discover positive qualities that have yet to be developed. There is little doubt that the relationship between parent and child is the most important influence on the young person's eventual view of himself.

Life is by design a series of changes. We are not meant to be victims of our past histories. Rather, the experiences of life can teach us to live positively in an imperfect world. The perspective the parent has of life in general, and of himself in particular, colors the way in which he interacts with his child. A young person reared in a home with positive parental leadership has a greater probability of developing a healthy view of himself and the life before him.

Words take a backseat to behavior.

    I have talked with many frustrated parents who complain how difficult it is to understand a child's reaction to parental leadership. Even though the parents try to be consistent in discipline, they continue to be challenged by a relentless child.

    We all have been told that actions speak louder than words. This simple truth provides the framework for a necessary parental guideline. We must recognize that children "read" the emotions behind our words and actions as they interpret our messages to them. For example:

- A parent may severely chastise a child for not completing a chore that had been assigned earlier in the day. The parent's desire is to evoke a sense of shame in the child that will motivate him to correct his irresponsibility. The child, though, may see the parent's remark as one in a long line of criticisms. He may feel incapable of pleasing his parent and thus make excuses, give a half-hearted effort, or only begrudgingly do as he is told.

- As a child faces the pressure of an upcoming exam in school, his mother becomes increasingly anxious about the grade the child may make if he does not study hard. Offering to help the child prepare for his exam, the mother is exasperated because the child seems to have little concern over how he will do on the upcoming test. The child, however, has learned that in such situations, he need not worry since his mother will take control of the responsibility, leaving him to assume a carefree attitude toward life.

- After being challenged by his teenage son, a father retorts, "Don't be concerned about my bad habits. That's not what we are focusing upon. You are to follow a few simple rules around here and one of the rules is that you may not smoke cigarettes while you are living in this house! Is that clear?" The son mumbles that he understands the rules, but thinks to himself that there is no way he intends to change his behavior as long as his dad has equally bad habits. He thinks of his father as a hypocrite.

A theme that runs throughout the scriptures is that of the value attached to human life. Though God frequently needed to deal harshly with the Israelites, it was never in a way that was demeaning to their character as individuals. There are countless reminders in the Bible of God's unwavering love for His human creation. The message must consistently be conveyed to our children that each person's worth as an individual is permanently fixed.

Of all the guidelines a parent must follow in providing leadership for the family, matching words with behavior is perhaps the most basic. It is also the most difficult to achieve. As we interact with our children, it is important to understand how our behavior and words are seen and interpreted by the child. By objectively analyzing our responses to the child, it is possible to more consistently balance the words that are spoken with the emotions, attitudes, and opinions that are expressed more subtly. Such underlying messages dominate our parent–child communications.

Use positive methods in guiding your child's behavior.

Although it is not always a conscious process, a child continually evaluates the interaction he has with others. As the child considers the effects of his chosen behavior, he learns about himself. Because children and adolescents are limited in their experience in life simply by virtue of their youth, it logically follows that many of the choices made during these formative years will not be wise ones. It is through the interaction the child has with his world that he eventually develops a stronger capacity for sound judgment and common sense.

The parent can provide a learning environment for the child that can minimize the negative consequences of the young person's relative lack of wisdom. The way parents react to the child has a powerful effect on the way in which that child chooses to continue to behave. For example:

- An infant child may learn to associate sitting in a parent's lap with the hugs that invariably follow, leading him to want to be physically near that parent.

- A primary school child may learn that when he does his chores as requested, increased responsibility and privileges are given.

- A preadolescent may learn that parents give permission for social activities if they are fully informed of the child's plans.

- A teenager may receive more spending money from parents after he displays financial responsibility.

When a child learns that positive things happen when he has behaved in a given way, there is a tendency for the young person to repeat that behavior. I find it interesting to observe children and their parents as the child searches for ways to gain approval from his Mom or Dad. The single reward a child wants most is attention. The need to feel recognized, approved, affirmed, and encouraged by the acknowledgement of a significant person is the greatest psychological need of a child. As simple as that statement may seem, it provides profound guidance to any parent in search of those essential truths that will help him shape the direction of his child's life.

As you interact with your own child, or as you observe other parents with their children, notice the intensity of the child's need to be noticed by the most significant adult in his life. It is a given fact that the child will in some way gain the attention of the parent. One child may have learned to get attention through clinging to his parent. A second child may gather attention through the use of whining or even tantrum behavior. Others, however, may learn that they are most frequently recognized when they follow directions, display courtesy, or cooperate with others.

Since the parent is the most significant person in the child's world, *it is essential for that adult to accept responsibility for guiding the child in a positive direction through life.* In many families where a child's behavior is out of control, the missing element is the of positive interaction between parent and child. The child may have learned that only negative behavior is rewarded with the parent's attention.

It is the parent who, by virtue of his leadership position, must actively determine to provide attention to the developing young personality. To fail to satisfy this basic psychological need of the child can lead to emotional pain that is difficult to heal.

Punishment procedures should be used wisely.

It is inevitable that you as parent will be required to punish your child on given occasions. While I strongly urge parents to search for ways to teach responsible behavior to children through the use of rewards whenever possible, there are times in which punishment is required and even recommended.

Many parents I have counseled report being dismayed to find themselves punishing their child far more frequently than they prefer to do. Furthermore, they feel their efforts to be fruitless. It is important to understand the use of punishment as a behavior management technique and how to use it effectively.

When a child is punished, the intent is to cause his negative behavior to decrease. Yet, in many instances it seems that punishment only makes matters worse. For example:

- Rather than complete her homework assignment after school, a daughter deliberately ignores this responsibility even though she has been grounded repeatedly for shirking her duty.

- Following a sound spanking and firm scolding, a preschooler defiantly throws a temper tantrum that lasts almost an hour.

- In response to their teenage son's violations of his Friday night curfew, parents take away his car keys for the remainder of the weekend. Late the next night the youth slips out of the house and drives his car without permission.

Punishment:	Child's Thought:	Result:
grounded	*I give up.*	irresponsibility
spanking	*I'll get even.*	defiance
car keys taken	*I'll outwit them.*	deceitfulness

A theme that will run throughout this book is the requirement of viewing life from the reference point of the child. By doing so, the parent can more clearly evaluate the effect of his reaction to the child. For example, a response intended by the parent as a punishment may be perceived by the child as a reward. Many oppositional children are reinforced by the frustration they create in a parent who has attempted to exert control through the use of punishment procedures. Even though that child may have to accept a negative consequence, its effect is slight compared to the odd sort of enjoyment gained from creating emotional turmoil within the parent.

As leader of the family, the parent must regularly determine the effectiveness of any behavior management techniques that are utilized. The goal is to guide the child in a desirable direction. Should self–evaluation reveal the use of punishment to such a degree that family relations are strained more often than improved, the following review of the proper use of punishment procedures may be helpful.

- Punishment should be administered with emotional control. A display of strong emotions at such a time creates opportunities for the child to engage in power struggle tactics.

- The child should be informed in advance of behaviors that will result in punishment. Arguing over rules and expectations should be avoided once disciplinary action is taken.

- Never use punishment without also using abundant rewards for acceptable behavior. A child should be rewarded at least twice as often as he is punished.

- Display a high degree of consistency in controlling behaviors that have been targeted for change.

- Refrain from using punishments that involve aggression if at all possible. An aggressive reaction (e.g. spanking, squeezing the arm strongly, exaggerated gestures, yelling) may teach the child to also display aggression when he is angry or upset.

- Use the minimum punishment necessary to make the desired point. Harsh and lengthy punishments are difficult for both the parent and child to endure. Parental inconsistency or childhood rebellion could result.

Few parents enjoy the role of disciplinarian. Certainly children can and should periodically be given punishment as a way of guiding them toward responsible behavior. Yet use of punishment procedures should never be the primary method of altering a child's behavior. The use of rewards aimed at directing the young person in a positive direction is far better to help the child establish a sense of worth and see the parent as an ally rather than an adversary. Only after a child feels his parents truly have his best interests at heart, will well–timed use of punishment techniques prove to be effective.

The Old Testament writer tells us that, "as a man disciplines his son, so the Lord your God disciplines you" (Deut. 8:5). Implied in this statement is the realization that love and discipline can coexist. Our loving God considers discipline to be necessary at times. The aim of the parent should be to enforce punishment in such a way that a child can eventually see it as an act of love.

Parents must give meaning to the child's life.

As I talked casually with a friend one day, he told me of feeling a certain amount of discouragement in his role as a parent. He felt an emptiness in his life and worried that he was encouraging the same lack of purpose in his two children. He noted that the most important things in the lives of his children centered around such things as the clothes they wore, social recognition, peer group status, and the accumulation of wealth. Even though others evaluated his family in a positive way, this father felt he had somehow failed to instill in his children a stronger understanding of life's meaning.

I congratulated my friend for the insight he had in examining his role as a family leader. I also encouraged him to alter his own personal and spiritual objectives to include goals aimed at personal fulfillment instead of those designed primarily to enhance personal status and material accumulation.

It is easy for adults to become burdened with a life–style that is emotionally bland. The desire for parents to provide for children's physical needs can encourage an overemphasis on offering children the "good life" to the detriment of meeting their needs for personal growth. Similarly, the need to provide disciplinary control may push the parent into overemphasizing this responsibility while overlooking the child's need for a relationship that teaches him about life's ultimate truths.

A major responsibility of the parent is to teach the child that each human life is of value and each individual can find that value through engaging in activities that have purpose. The parent can provide valuable guidance as the young person embarks on a lifelong process of fulfilling the capabilities that make him a unique person.

As leader of the family, the parent is the primary figure the child looks to for direction in meeting life's demands. The parent who is well on the way to his own personal fulfillment may offer a model by which the child can pattern his life. I like to view life as an ongoing process in which we never reach a point of completion. Yet, parents who have the greatest effect on the personal growth of their children display many of the following characteristics:

- An acceptance of individual differences which aids in tolerating behaviors that are different than those he would choose.

- A perception of personal strengths and weaknesses within himself. Shortcomings are recognized and efforts are made to improve upon them.

- Confidence, but not to the point of feeling superior to others.

- A problem–solving attitude which allows decisions to be made rationally rather than emotionally when facing dilemmas.

- Religious convictions that are firm but are not pushed upon others with a zeal that is offensive.

- A sense of enjoyment of the little things in life.

- A balanced empathy for others that is expressed with neither too little nor too much concern.

- A few close friends who are preferred to an ever–widening circle of acquaintances.

- Humor that is displayed in a loving, not harmful, manner.

- Communication marked by clear messages that are without deceit or hidden motive.

One of the more frightening and simultaneously rewarding responsibilities of parenthood is that of providing guidance to the next generation of adults. Children have the remarkably challenging task of learning to correctly interpret their world, interact effectively with others, and discover the God–given value inherent in their very lives. They must also learn to work productively and develop an identity of who they are in a behavioral, emotional, and spiritual sense.

Bringing a child into a family brings unsurpassed joy to an adult's world. A task of parenthood is to give knowledge and guidance to a child with the hope of seeing that young person move toward reaching the substantial potential that is within him.

Study Session

Objective:

To determine your style of parental leadership and its effect on your child's behavior and emotional development.

Biblical Reference: Heb. 12:5–11

These verses provide an excellent explanation for the need of discipline in the Christian life. These words also offer a summary of the educational process the child goes through under the guiding hand of a parent.

Discussion Questions:

1. What leadership style do you display with your children? Are you controlling? Compromising? A "pushover"? What are the reasons you have developed this style of leadership?

2. What type of leadership needs are required by your children? How does your children's age, maturity level, and personality style affect the leadership style you display? How flexible are you in adjusting to the individual needs of your children?

3. How would your child describe your parenting style? Are the complaints he would make warranted? How well does your child understand the decisions you must make as a parent?

4. How does your own self-concept reflect the parenting style you display? Are you uncertain? Too dogmatic? Do you take out personal problems on your child?

5. What do you normally do when you want to change your child's behavior? Do you have a "plan of action"? Do you usually just do what comes naturally? How satisfied are you with the results you normally get?

6. What is your communication pattern with your child? Do you think your child feels you understand him? Do you allow for differing opinions? How open is the dialogue between you and your child?

Assignments:

1. Spend some time alone with your child. Tell him you are
    honestly evaluating your relationship with him. Ask for his
    opinion on what could be done to make the family get along
    better. Without being defensive or feeling a need to make a
    counter argument, just listen. Keep the topic open for dis-
    cussion for several days.

2. Do an assessment of yourself as a parent. Make a list of both
    your strengths and your weaknesses. Compare your own
    perception of yourself to the feedback your child has given you.

1

Let's Slug It Out—

The Oppositional Child

—Case Study—

IT SEEMED THAT THE REMINDERS came too often. Mr. and Mrs. Whiteside received frequent feedback from others that their 15–year–old daughter was difficult to manage. Just recently they had been called to attend a conference at Carolyn's school. They did not flinch as the counselor described Carolyn's tendency to talk back to her teachers. The word *sassy* was used several times to characterize her language.

Mr. and Mrs. Whiteside listened as the counselor cited examples of Carolyn's disregard for rules. Earlier in the day, Carolyn had created turmoil in one of her classrooms when she explained to her teacher in colorful language why she had not completed a simple assignment. The conflict between adolescent and adult began as a minor misunderstanding and ended in a loud tantrum by Carolyn which resulted in her expulsion from the classroom.

This latest reminder of Carolyn's disobedience sounded like a broken record to the Whitesides. Throughout her nine years in school they had been invited to numerous conferences with teachers, counselors, and principals. Complaints from neighbors were also common. Carolyn was forever insulting someone. Even her friends pegged her as being "different." They were intimidated, astonished, and embarrassed by her actions all at one time. Other teenagers were hesitant to develop too close a relationship with her since her moods changed so suddenly.

Nothing seemed to stop Carolyn's pattern of behavior. Her parents had tried everything they could think of to bring her actions under control. She certainly had received more than her share of spankings through the years. It seemed that she was forever grounded. Most of her material possessions had been withheld from her at one time or another. She disregarded lectures about the effects of her behavior on others. After 15 years of struggling, Carolyn's was still an enigma.

Defining the Oppositional Child

Our culture assumes that children will accept the guidance given to them by adults. Most children assert themselves from time to time in a show of independence. A few, however, are seemingly in constant conflict with authority figures. Arguments are begun even though there seems to be no plausible reason to fight. Cooperation is a word that is foreign to this child. Competition, even aggression, takes its place.

I believe oppositional behavior from children and adolescents has grown in its prevalence in the past generation, but as a pattern of behavior it has been present for centuries. Imagine the behavior pattern the Prodigal Son displayed prior to his demand that he be given his inheritance. A profile of this young man would quite likely yield many qualities of an oppositional child.

As difficult as this child is to manage, the oppositional child presents a consistent and predictable set of characteristics. Several common traits identify this child.

Challenges authority figures. The oppositional child enjoys being in control. To a child or adolescent, the adult represents the greatest barrier to being in a position of control. From a very young age the child senses his relative dependence upon adults. Most children take comfort in knowing that adults can be counted upon to provide guidance through life. But, the oppositional child is more likely to take offense at the adult's status.

There are numerous ways oppositional children and adolescents may challenge an adult's position of authority.

- An eight year old may refuse to come into the house when he hears his name called . . . for the third time . . . by his parent.

- An 18 month old may look his parent squarely in the eye as he opens a forbidden cabinet door.

- A 13–year–old girl may shout "I hate you!" when told that she has applied a bit too much makeup.

- A high school student may stay out two hours past his curfew, knowing that his father will be waiting for him when he arrives at home.

- A six year old may jeer and taunt his mother immediately following a tantrum.

Control is a very important word to the oppositional child. Because this young person is competitive, he strongly desires to be in charge of others. This child will assume he is as knowledgeable as any adult and is quick to challenge the parent's position of authority in the home.

Remains negative even though the negativism serves no purpose. Long after a reasonable negative reaction has been displayed, the oppositional child continues to hold on dearly to his "right" to be negative. Emotional expressions of anger are not readily dismissed. The child seems intent on maintaining a high level of emotion even though others around him have long since subdued theirs. His emotion serves little use other than to demonstrate his ability to choose to be stubborn.

There is a limited awareness in this young person of how improper his behavior appears to others. He is more concerned with asserting his assumed rights as a person than in properly controlling his negativism. He tends to interpret any attempt to subdue his emotions as a violation of his freedom to act as he pleases.

—Case Study—

Ronald and Cory fought all the way home from school over whether or not Ronald was allowed to keep the change from the lunch money he had received from his mother that morning. Ronald reasoned that Mother should be given the change only if she requested it. Otherwise, the money belonged to him.

As the brothers walked into their home, Cory immediately told Mother that Ronald had extra money that should be returned to her. Ronald became enraged and acted out a lively tantrum. Even after Mother took discipline matters into her own hands and corrected her son's behavior, he refused to dismiss his anger. He pouted all evening and grumbled whenever he was spoken to. He was especially harsh toward his brother. He refused to accept consolation from his parents and even declined the apology offered by Cory. Ronald's insistence on holding tightly to his anger ensured an uncomfortable evening for the entire family. And it could have been avoided by his willingness to discard an overworked emotion.

As depicted in Ronald's case, the oppositional child makes inappropriate use of his emotions (see figure 2). Because it is difficult for him to view life from any perspective other than his own, he fails to use good judgment in his emotional expression. Rather than assert his opinion when feeling the need to correct a situation, he allows his assertion to become aggression. The opportunity to be constructive turns into unnecessary destruction.

Prefers competition to cooperation. There is something exciting about competition. When we compete, there is an uncertainty about the eventual outcome of the event. The risks involved in competition are stimulating to many individuals. The competitive person willingly and confidently matches his skills against another's abilities. There is a certain feeling within the heart that anticipates an opportunity for victory.

The oppositional child uses the thrill of competition in an effort to gain an odd assortment of trophies:

- Conflict with others is provoked to cause others to feel frustrated.

- Emotional control of peers or adults feels powerful.

- Intimidation provides a strong sense of reinforcement.

- Attention—even if it is negative—provides incentive for arguments which serve no other useful purpose.

- Arguments may postpone, or even cancel, a showdown the child fears he will lose.

The oppositional child has a tendency to take a good trait and then overwork it to such a degree that it is no longer useful. Competitiveness can be a positive quality in a child. Such a child may be motivated to become all he is capable of being. A competitive drive may result in the successes that cause a child to feel good about his accomplishments. Without competition in his world, many of the positive capabilities within a child may never be adequately tapped.

However, competitiveness that is overworked generally results in aggression. Aggression can encourage a lack of sensitivity to the needs of others. It can blind a child to the good that can come from interacting in a cooperative way with others who may share the same goals in life.

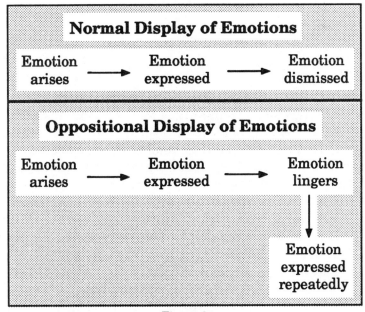

Figure 2

The oppositional child frequently will make the erroneous mistake of assuming that he can succeed in the world by acting alone. He believes that to involve others in a joint effort will only slow him down as he presses toward a desired goal. Unfortunately, when this child's goals are not met, the end result is often heightened competitive drive rather than an emphasis on a cooperative effort with others.

Right and wrong are determined by the consequence of a behavior. Most adults prefer to think of an action as being right if it serves a useful purpose and follows the rules our society has established as being reasonable. Behavior is considered to be wrong if it inflicts harm and violates the reasonable standards of our society.

The oppositional child is not guided by such a lofty level of moral ethics. In his way of thinking, if he gets caught with his hand in the cookie jar, then his behavior was wrong—maybe. If no one sees him snitch a cookie, then it was not wrong. This simple way of thinking prevents the oppositional child from feeling any real sense of guilt!

—Case Study—

Randy was a 16–year–old high school sophomore who did not have a high regard for school. It was his stated intention to refrain from ever reading a book following his graduation from high school. One Friday afternoon Randy made the decision to skip his last two classes to get a head start on the weekend.

As Randy was driving into a local fast food establishment, he had the misfortune of seeing his father pass by in his car. The hope that Dad did not see him quickly faded as Randy saw his father wheel his car around to meet him in the parking lot of the restaurant. A confrontation was inevitable.

"School didn't end early today, did it, Randy?"

"No."

"Then what are you doing here? Your class going on a field trip to see how hamburgers are made?"

"Quit bugging me, Dad. I didn't feel like going to class so I left school a little early. It's no big deal, you know. It's not like I'm the only one in the world who's ever skipped school."

"No big deal? How do you expect to get an education if you don't attend school? I'd say it's a pretty big deal!"

"Dad, we weren't doing anything in either of my classes. In history we were just going to watch a film and in English I think they were going to do something I already know how to do. And besides, nobody will ever know I'm gone. They'll just think I got sick. Nobody checks the attendance roll that closely."

"That's not the point, son. The point is that your responsibility is to attend school all day, not just when you feel like going. It's *wrong* to skip school. You know that."

"What do you mean *wrong*! Nobody even knows I'm gone. How can that be wrong?"

With that statement, Randy engaged his father in a cycle of words over the rightness or wrongness of his action. Randy based his argument on the hope that the authority figures at school would remain ignorant of his whereabouts. Dad pleaded a case based on the educational harm that could result from poor attendance habits and on the value of keeping the rules he was obligated to follow because he was a student.

The argument ended with Randy having his car keys taken away for several days. Yet, even though Randy received punishment, Dad was not at all convinced his son had learned a lesson about his need for school attendance. Randy simply looked at things in a peculiar manner! Dad even questioned his son's intelligence. Surely no smart teenager would think as Randy did.

A more mature adult is more likely to view right and wrong based on a higher level of reasoning than an oppositional child. There is a self–centered quality to the strong–willed young person that persuades him from seeing a situation from any viewpoint other than his own. The dogmatic insistence by the oppositional child to judge his actions primarily on the subsequent consequences and not upon sound reasoning is fuel for many arguments between parent and child.

Fails to respond to normal discipline measures. A mother once told me that her daughter responded well to discipline, but her son was a completely different story. Mother never knew how he would react to discipline. Her plan was simple. If her children behaved well, she rewarded them. If they broke the rules of the family, they received punishment. Her daughter understood the guidelines of the family and responded in a predictable way. The only prediction she would make about her son was that he would be unpredictable.

Because the oppositional child views life in a self–centered way, he attaches his own value to the rewards and punishments rendered to him. He may disregard an intended reward that another child would relish. He shrugs off the effect of an apparently strong punishment.

When honest, the oppositional child will shed light on what he considers to be either rewarding or punishing. His definition of these terms is unique. A reward might be:

- The reputation of being "bad."

- The excitement of a good fight.

- The opportunity to make another person feel uncomfortable.

- The powerful feeling of intimidation.

- The attention of others, even if it is negative.

A punishment might be:

- The refusal of another person to argue.

- The loss of control resulting from others withdrawing from his presence.

- Lack of interaction with others.

- Not being allowed to call the shots.

The oppositional child becomes aware at an early age that others do not always recognize his unique way of responding to normal discipline procedures. Being the personality type that seizes upon opportunities, he exploits the lack of understanding others have of him. He enjoys having the knowledge that others look upon him as mysterious because of his unorthodox reaction to discipline.

As I talked with one oppositional boy about this very matter, he explained to me, "My Mom and Dad think they know how I really think, but they don't. They think I'm upset when they ground me from going out with my friends. Don't get me wrong, I do like being with my friends. But, I really don't care if I'm punished, because I know they're just as upset as I am. That makes my punishment worth it."

This young man provided a valuable insight into the way an oppositional child thinks. He is unconventional in his reaction to normal responses his behavior will elicit from adults. Knowing that most adults have difficulty comprehending his way of behaving, this youngster fully exploits the confusion he has created in his effort to control others.

Factors Influencing the Oppositional Child's Behavior

Inborn disposition. In the same way that other behavioral characteristics may be a part of a child's inborn tendency, the penchant toward a difficult behavior pattern may be present from a very early age. In a group of toddlers, the oppositional child can be readily spotted. He will be the one barking instructions to his playmates. He will lead the charge onto the playground equipment. He will cry angrily when his drink is accidentally kicked over. Adults will call his name more frequently than the other children's names. As the child grows older, his behavior may take on various forms, but the underlying dynamics are still present.

—Case Study—

Belinda's mother was tired after 17 years of battling her daughter. She stated with exasperation that Belinda's journey from infancy through adolescence had not been easy. She chronicled her child's behavioral development.

- By the time she was two, Belinda had already shown her tendency to argue and struggle with others over petty matters. Mother had heard of the "terrible two's," but Belinda gave new meaning to the term. It was then that she developed a strong preference for the word *no*.

- The elementary school years saw Belinda become more frequently involved in conflicts with other children. She developed a reputation as the toughest girl in the school. All too often she became embroiled in disputes with adults and other students that caused her to be criticized and punished more than would be normally expected.

- The preadolescent years were especially trying. It was a struggle to get Belinda to complete any of her simple responsibilities. Even though she was intellectually bright, she did not put much effort into her schoolwork. She argued constantly with Mother about how much time she should spend on the telephone, the amount of makeup she should wear, and how much time she had to spend practicing the piano.

- During adolescence the roof fell in. Belinda snuck out to meet her boyfriend late at night. She showed open disregard for her parents and their authority. She drifted into periodic alcohol abuse. When encouraged to make plans for life after high school, she would only state that she wanted to get out of the house and be on her own.

Chronicle of Belinda's Behavior	
Age	Oppositional Behavior
2 yrs.	struggles with authority
5–10 yrs.	argues with peers and adults
11–13 yrs.	irresponsible; self-absorbed
14–17 yrs.	out of control; no regard for rules

Figure 3

Though the symptoms of Belinda's oppositional behavior changed as she advanced through the stages of childhood and adolescence, there was a common thread running throughout her development. Each age saw its own expression of negativism, argumentativeness, and belligerence that had roots reaching back to her very early years in which her temperament was first displayed.

Many frustrated parents of oppositional children have asked me to help them examine ways they might have inadvertently caused their children to develop such difficult patterns of behavior. I encourage these parents to release themselves from the grip of guilt that strangles them. A true oppositional child would be a challenge for any parent to raise. Certainly this young person may have pushed the parent into erroneous actions, but his own disposition is at the root of many of his rebellious acts. The parent who relieves himself from the responsibility of his child's natural temperament is in a stronger position to effectively manage that child.

Oppositional behavior can be reinforced. As we have noted, the oppositional child frequently does not respond to discipline measures in a conventional manner. In fact, many confrontations with this child turn into victories for him. These victories provide incentive for further arguments. Thus, an argument becomes a potential opportunity for the oppositional child to feel rewarded.

To understand how arguments can be reinforcing, we must look (from the child's point of view) at what it is about confrontations that are rewarding. Two key words quickly surface. Those words are *control* and *power*.

All individuals like to feel that they have a certain sense of control in their lives. A child likes to feel that his life is in order. It has consistency. He can predict what is likely to happen next. The feeling of control gives a sense of security.

Because the child is less experienced and more developmentally immature than his parents, it is the parent who should provide the child with the sense of security that comes from a controlled home environment. As the child grows to maturity, the reins of control should gradually be given to him. All too often the child tries to take over the control of himself too quickly, leading to monumental mistakes. While mistakes make up an important part of growing up, the parent wants to ensure that his child's errors are not too costly.

The oppositional child tends to want to take charge of all of his own decisions sooner than he is able to responsibly do so. When parents place barriers before him to prevent the harm that would inevitably arise from the child's lack of judgment, the child looks for other ways to satisfy the desire to be in control. In most cases, the frustrated oppositional child attempts to gain control through emotional tactics. That is, he takes charge of the emotions of the adult. The sense of control experienced by a child who feels emotionally in charge of an adult is strongly rewarding.

Along with the feeling of being in control, the oppositional child feels a strong sense of power. He enjoys being able to dictate to an adult the mood he will take on. He begins to feel that adults have no authority over him. The surge of control and power encourages the oppositional child to be overly assertive and even aggressive.

—Case Study—

At age 11, Jarrell was becoming increasingly irresponsible in his school performance. He had always been at least average in school, but as a sixth grader he made his first failing grades on a report card. His parents were quite naturally concerned and intended to take measures to help him improve his grades. They announced to Jarrell that each day following school he was to complete his work prior to playing with friends, watching television, or any other enjoyable activity. Jarrell responded indifferently.

Over the next two weeks, Jarrell frequently failed to follow the instructions his parents had given him. Before his parents could see his homework, he was on the telephone with a friend or down the block on his bicycle. A series of confrontations between Jarrell and his parents ensued. As his parents became more frustrated and upset, they threatened to be even more stringent in their punishment. They reminded him of the new telephone he wanted for his room and told him that he would not receive it without an improvement in his grades. Their emotional patience with him was obviously wearing thin.

Jarrell reacted by becoming more defiant. Instead of cooperating with his parents, he became more hostile. He hurled his own accusations at his parents. He accused them of not caring about him. He stated that he hoped he failed the sixth grade because he did not want to do what someone else told him to do.

Who was in control of the environment of this home? Jarrell was. He recognized that he could force his own irresponsible decisions upon his parents. Their reaction of exasperation and anger let him know that it was he who decided their emotional state.

He liked that feeling. So much did he enjoy the joint feelings of control and power that he unwisely decided that continued school failure was of little concern.

The combined feeling of being in control of his parents' emotions and its accompanying power was rewarding to Jarrell. By inadvertently giving him the opportunity to be in charge, his parents increased the likelihood that he would continue his argumentative and stubborn behavior.

Oppositional behavior may be imitated. There are times that both good news and bad news are contained in the same message. Such is the case in the statement that many childhood behaviors are learned by observing adults. The good news is that the parent is in a prime position to model the type of behavior desired in the child. The bad news is that the child may very well learn a few things about oppositional behavior by observing his parents.

—Case Study—

Becky's mother expressed concern over Becky's increasingly unmanageable behavior. Mother described a battle that had recently occurred. The previous Friday night Becky had come home at her normal curfew hour. However, about 30 minutes later, Mother discovered that the teenager had left the house and made her way down the street to be with three of her unruly friends. Naturally angered, Mother aroused Becky's father from bed and insisted that the two of them confront their daughter and bring her home.

As soon as Becky's parents reached the cluster of girls, Mother exploded. "Just what do you think you're doing out here at this hour of the night? You know you're supposed to be in bed asleep by now! And you girls, do your parents know where you are? Well, they will when I get home because I'm calling them on the phone!"

Mother grabbed Becky by the arm demanding that she come home. Becky struck back at her mother as the fight was now in full force. Dad helplessly tried to intervene but was unable to terminate the argument. It was not until an hour had passed that Mother and daughter set aside their verbal weapons and went to bed. Neither slept well that night.

Listening to Becky alone in my office, she told me how similar arguments were common in her household. She readily admitted that her behavior was not always exemplary, but added that it was very hard for her to turn away from a good fight. She further stated that her mother was of no help in bringing these conflicts under control. Becky was probably right in expressing that she had learned many of her argumentative ways from her mother.

In my experience of observing children, I have yet to observe a child display argumentative and confrontive behavior when he is all alone. His abrasive behavior is always directed at someone. Quite commonly that individual is the parent. Not only does the parent's willingness to butt heads with the child provide opportunities for the child to take control of the emotional atmosphere, it also offers the child a model of how to handle adversity—by arguing! Once the parent has been enticed into an argument, he often will use tactics that will resurface in the child's own behavioral repertoire. These include:

- Making threats that will not be carried out.

- Bringing up past events rather than focusing on the present.

- Shouting and yelling to make a point.

- Interrupting while the child is talking.

- Starting sentences with phrases such as, "You always . . . " or "You never . . . "

- Withholding affection from the child.

- Trying to force an opinion on the child.

Many additional reactions could be added to the list of behaviors that could be modeled for the child. Regardless of the child's age, he tends to recall experiences with a parent when reacting to a potentially confrontive situation. Often the same tactics used by the parent to confront oppositional behavior will resurface in the child's own behavior.

Failed communication may encourage oppositional behavior. I have heard countless oppositional children and adolescents voice the complaint that no one understands their feelings. Despite their vocal and forceful natures, these children often feel alone with their thoughts and emotions. Once the oppositional child develops trust in another person, he will often talk of the desire for improved relationships with others. He may even state that he becomes verbally aggressive because he knows of no other way to make his feelings known. Disruptive behavior may escalate when the young person feels the need to communicate his emotions. Unable to adequately express his feelings through words, he expresses himself through his behavior, albeit inappropriate behavior.

The most important skill in communication is that of *listening*. Listening involves more than merely hearing the words that another person has spoken. The most vital function of listening is to accurately interpret the message being expressed. Listening accurately to an oppositional child can be difficult because of the aggressive way he communicates with others.

An oppositional child is by nature an opinionated child. He frequently experiences intense emotions as well. It stands to reason, then, that when the oppositional child makes a statement there are many implied thoughts and emotions below the surface of his spoken words. When this child is not able to adequately express all that is within him, his emotional intensity rises.

Often it is difficult to know how to respond to a child who has just made a highly emotional statement. There are many potential responses to make to the oppositional child. Some are more helpful than others. Some responses actually encourage further angry impulses and should be avoided. The oppositional child is quick to notice a verbal reaction that fails to communicate an understanding of his point of view. Here are some common harmful communication responses:

- A neighbor spotted an eight–year–old boy throwing rocks through the garage window of an unoccupied house and informed the boy's father. In turn, the father confronted the boy with this information.

  "Kyle, Mr. Ritter told me he saw you throwing rocks through the windows of the empty house down the street. Do you have anything to say about it?"

  "It's none of Mr. Ritter's business. Tell him to leave me alone!"

"Kyle, it is Mr. Ritter's business. I'd want to know if a boy were vandalizing my house. I demand an answer!"

"Hey, who does he think he is anyway, the police? How would you like it if someone went around spying on you all the time and told your dad everything you did wrong. It's not fair!"

By trying to gain a confession of guilt from Kyle, Dad was doomed to frustration. Rather than cooperate with his father, Kyle looked for a way to place fault on Mr. Ritter. Father and son were moving in two different directions. The more they talked, the farther apart they drifted from each other.

- A child hurried into the house to find her mother and immediately complained, "Mom, Richard and Jim are being rude! They make up all the rules when we play kickball and never let me say what I think. I can't stand them!"

  Mom reacted quickly by trying to redirect her daughter's attention. "Well, why don't you stay here with me and we'll work on cleaning up your room. We've needed to do that for several days now anyway."

  Mom was not greeted with the response she hoped for. "Clean up my room? Why? I don't need to clean up my room!" She then stomped out of the house to continue her play feeling that none of her problems were resolved.

Mom had assumed that if her daughter was kept busy, she would forget about her problem. By attempting to divert the girl's attention, Mom conveyed the message that she did not want to be involved in the problem her daughter had experienced with her peers. The girl was left feeling that her needs were not shown proper respect.

- William had been chastised by his girlfriend for always being late to pick her up whenever they were to go anywhere. The youth mentioned to his father that he did not understand his girlfriend's need for punctuality. It was William's opinion that promptness was not that important since few events actually went according to the planned schedule.

  William's father secretly agreed with the girlfriend. He also liked the girl and didn't want to see his son lose a relationship because of his irresponsibility. He warned William, "You'd better watch it or you may lose a girlfriend. Besides, you could probably learn something from her."

"I should have known you'd say something like that. You never see things the way I do." William was offended.

Dad had predicted what might happen to William if he did not take greater care to consider his girlfriend's wishes. Though Dad may have been correct, William took offense at his father's prediction and withdrew from his presence without a sense of emotional release.

- Julia was in an unusually thoughtful mood and remarked to her mother, "I'm getting sick of fighting with everybody. Sometimes I don't think anyone likes me."

  Julia's mother thought she had an opportune moment to teach Julia how others perceive her. "Julia, when you fight with people all the time, of course they won't like you. Remember when you were fighting with Ramona yesterday when she was here at our house? Do you think she liked you then? I don't."

  "Don't blame me for that, Mom! You know how Ramona is always looking for a good fight. That wasn't my fault!"

Mother had said nothing untrue. Julia knew that, but did not wish to bear any greater guilt about her behavior. Mother had posed a thoughtful statement, but utilized poor timing. Julia was not prepared for constructive criticism. Her desire at the moment was to feel understood. Instead of feeling helped, she felt a sense of judgment.

I believe that communication is the most important tool a parent has in controlling oppositional behavior. Failure to communicate appropriately with an argumentative child creates further rebellion and negative emotions within that child.

Power struggles may encourage continued oppositional behavior. Management of the oppositional child is difficult to achieve for many parents because most of the struggles between this child and his parents are on an emotional level. So often a conflict arises over a petty matter and becomes a major event because the focus shifts from an identifiable problem to one that is covert. The struggle for power and control becomes fierce.

In most cases, the parent tends to search for a punishment that is sufficiently strong enough to convince the oppositional child to relinquish his stubborn position and act appropriately. The child recognizes the dilemma of the parent and stubbornly refuses to be changed through the use of punishment techniques.

Control of a child's oppositional behavior can be achieved only with an understanding of the nature of the power struggle. A grasp of the dynamics of this exchange can tremendously aid the parent in managing the oppositional child.

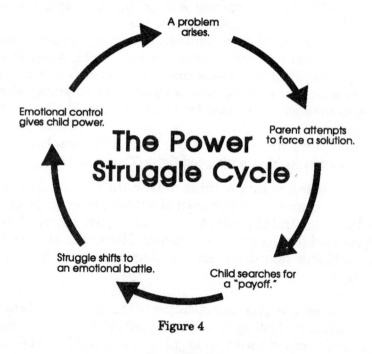

Figure 4

—*Case Study*—

One of Judy's daily responsibilities was to clean her lunch box and put it away each afternoon upon her return home from school. Mother was forever fussing at Judy, threatening to put her lunch in a brown paper sack if she found that her lunch box was unclean. Judy typically responded by arguing with her mother.

She frequently warned her mother that she had better not send her to school carrying her lunch in a paper sack.

Finally, Mother decided to follow through with her promised action and presented Judy's lunch to her one morning in a brown paper sack. Mother explained that the lunch box would be used again when Judy decided to clean it. Admittedly, Mother felt a sense of vindication as she told her daughter what to expect from her. To her surprise, Judy agreed to the terms spelled out by her mother and took her lunch to school in the dreaded sack.

Each afternoon for three consecutive days Mother said nothing as Judy persistently refused to clean her lunch box. Unable to contain her anger any longer, Mother blew up at Judy after the third day and once again revived the battle over her daughter's neglect of her responsibility.

There are four elements contained in a power struggle. They are:

1. A problem presents itself—such as a dirty lunch box needing to be cleaned.

2. The parent takes on the problem and tries to resolve it by forcing a solution.

3. The child searches for a way to gain a payoff from the situation. He attempts to overcome the power displayed by the parent.

4. The struggle shifts from an obvious, identifiable problem to one that is hidden or covert. That is, the struggle is no longer for behavioral control, but for emotional control.

It is important to note that the child may lose the struggle for behavioral control but still win the power struggle. In the case study above, Judy lost the struggle for behavioral control in that she had to carry her lunch in a brown paper sack. Yet, she won the struggle for emotional control since she was well aware of her mother's building frustration as a result of her refusal to clean her lunch box.

The oppositional child is greatly rewarded by the knowledge that he has controlled the atmosphere in the home. It is a powerful feeling to know that Mother, Dad, and even Brother and Sister act as they do because of what the oppositional member of the family has done. Judy received her reward when after three days of keeping her thoughts to herself, Mother finally exploded.

Negative effects of the power struggle. The oppositional child typically does not consider the long–range effects of his own behavior. More than other children and adolescents, he looks predominantly at the present and its temporary rewards. Therefore, it is important for the parent to recognize the harmful side effects of becoming repeatedly involved in power struggles with this child.

Frequent involvement in power struggles encourages further oppositional behavior. An oppositional child will quickly recognize a parent's tendency to fall prey to power tactics and will take advantage of this developing pattern. After a short period of time, the feeling of control becomes strong, almost to the point of addiction. As the child grows older he becomes willing to go to more extreme measures to avoid giving up the power he has attained. His ability to be in charge becomes a part of his self–image. To lose control would be equivalent to losing a part of his "self."

—Case Study—

When William was a preschooler, he was known as a child who had a difficult temperament. He was quite demanding and cried when he did not get his way. His father tended to be rather strict with him and was able to stay away from parent–child confrontations. His mother, however, could not tolerate his crying spells and frequently gave in to his requests.

For several years, Mom maintained a relatively good relationship with William. She kept peace in the house by seeing to it that her son was satisfied. When William was nine years old, his parents divorced. William and his younger brother remained in the custody of their mother. Without his father's presence, William knew that he could now gain complete control of the household. Using tactics that he knew would bring success, he made demands that became increasingly difficult for his mother to fulfill.

When William was 12 years old, Mother determined that she must regain control of her family. She actively resisted William's attempts to do as he pleased. He retaliated by frustrating her to tears. An intelligent boy, he was aware of the limits of his mother's tolerance—and he always succeeded in pushing her one step beyond that boundary.

Mother sought help at my office. William told me that he did not enjoy the frequent arguing with his mother. He felt a sense of guilt over his negative behavior. He knew he had developed a reputation as the black sheep of the family, and he was angry at being punished constantly.

Yet, William freely admitted that he did not want to relinquish his position of authority within his family. A pattern had been established which he did not want to reverse. To voluntarily relinquish control was the equivalent of denouncing himself to the entire world. Such humiliation was more than this 12–year–old child could bear. To break the long chain of struggles for power, William needed to rely on his mother to make the first move. To do otherwise would be a great defeat.

Other undesirable behaviors may develop to compliment oppositional behavior. Because the oppositional child craves power, he is quick to learn which behaviors draw a response from the parent that leads to control. Through trial and error, he learns how to bait the adult. In many cases, the oppositional child can start a good struggle simply by arguing. But, the resourceful child will use many other devices to prove his control. These include:

- Intentionally ignoring a simple command.
- Making poor grades in school.
- Displaying poor manners in front of others.
- Telling lies or half–truths.
- Withdrawing while the adult is speaking.
- Teasing a sibling.
- Resorting to name–calling and sarcasm.
- Making threats—and following through with them.

The list of methods useful to the oppositional child goes on and on. Each child learns over the course of time which behaviors will solicit the reaction he desires from the adult. Though the tactics may vary from child to child, the end result is predictably similar. The oppositional child also becomes an irresponsible child.

He has concluded that it is not necessary for him to be responsible for his actions. As planned, the parent has taken that burden from him. The child has won the struggle for power.

Managing the Oppositional Child

Because the parent is the logical leader of the household, it holds that redirecting oppositional behavior must begin with a change in management styles. The oppositional child has probably learned that discipline approaches which rely heavily upon intimidation, fear, criticism, or punishment can be overcome. Being a child who enjoys a good argument, he has learned to turn the tables and use confrontation to his own advantage.

By looking at oppositional behavior from the child's perspective, the parent can recognize the benefits provided to the child when he falls prey to the child's game plan. While the parent does not cause the child's misbehavior, he may be inadvertently encouraging it by his reactions. Changing those reactions are important in managing the behavior of the oppositional child.

Emotions must be properly controlled. The key to disengaging from the oppositional child's problem lies in the control of emotions. As noted before, this child is quick to detect the anger, frustration, embarrassment, or disappointment he has evoked from his parent. He is equally swift to utilize these emotions as the tools for building his base of control.

A child cannot functionally punish his parents. He cannot ground his mother from the TV set, or make her stay home on Saturday night. He cannot take away his father's car keys or forbid him to go out with a friend on a social engagement. But, the oppositional child recognizes that he *can* make his parents feel angry, exasperated, or ashamed. The emotions of the adult are the only weapons a child can employ in his bid for power and control. And I might add, they are quite effective weapons.

To avoid becoming trapped in a power struggle with the oppositional child, the parent must develop a healthy sense of detachment from the problem behaviors of the child. The child must learn that the adult has no stake in the problem at hand. The child must retain the responsibility to solve that dilemma.

Paul wisely counsels us, "In your anger do not sin" (Eph. 4:26). Often the parent will mistakenly assume that to properly control his emotions, they must be ignored or somehow held in check as an attempt is made to effectively respond to a child's behavior. Yet Paul's counsel suggests that it is appropriate to be upset at times, provided proper boundaries are placed around our emotions.

I do not advocate that a parent hide his emotions from the child. To try to do so would be an impossibility. The oppositional child is perceptive and can detect when he is in the presence of an adult whose blood is near the boiling point. It is necessary to adopt a philosophy of behavior management that allows the oppositional child to make mistakes. Thus, the change made in reaction to problem situations does *not* necessarily focus upon what is *done* in response to the behavior, but in *how* that response is made and in the *attitude* in which that reaction is given.

Boundaries must be provided. To effectively manage the oppositional child, the child must maintain responsibility for his own behavior. It is he who must come to his own conclusions about the wisdom of his own behavior. To try to force conclusions, opinions, or facts upon the child simply prolongs oppositional behavior. Yet the child cannot be expected to show proper judgment in all decision–making opportunities. In fact, a major reason the oppositional child so frequently finds himself in conflict is his lack of reasoning and common sense.

Because the parent is the leader of the home, it is his proper position to provide guidance to the child. Since the oppositional child does not want specific guidance in many matters, the parent must then offer a set of choices that provide boundaries within which the child may act. If mistakes are made by the child, the previously stated boundaries will more likely provide a safeguard against disastrous judgmental errors. The child is allowed to learn from the mistakes he has made.

Examples of the boundaries parents can place around the oppositional child are:

- Poor grades in school result in completing homework before other activities. Good grades allow the child a choice in his own afternoon schedule.

- Coming in late on a weekend night results in an earlier curfew the following weekend. Promptness equates to greater flexibility in determining curfew times.

- Emotional outbursts cause the child to be isolated in a room alone. Emotional control will allow the child freedom to express varied points of view.

- Telling lies will cause the parent to make all decisions about the necessary consequences of the child's actions. Being truthful about misbehavior will allow for greater flexibility and input from the child.

Many parents tell me that similar boundaries have been provided to their child, yet behaviors still rage out of control. Through conversations with oppositional children and teenagers, I have gained insight to explain why firm boundaries become loose and ineffective.

The oppositional child observes the parent closely to determine if the adult is truly serious in his intention to stick to the guidelines that have been stated. The parent's inability to consistently remain within the established boundaries suggests to the oppositional child that the parent has taken the child's problems as his own. Thus, with the responsibility for decision–making taken from him, the oppositional child is free to continue his argumentative ways.

—Case Study—

Bryan, age 12, never did like school. When he first entered kindergarten, he often cried when his mother took him to school. Somehow, she always managed to coax him into the building. As he grew older, Bryan went through periods of time when he argued with his mother about attending school. Though becoming more difficult to manage, Bryan never missed a day of school for reasons other than legitimate illness.

This day was different. Intent on taking a vacation day from his studies, Bryan dug in his heels. As he and his mother rounded the corner to approach the school, Bryan began his resistance. He complained of a stomachache. He then slandered his teacher, saying he did not like her. Next, he argued that his classmates made fun of him and never included him in their activities.

After becoming weary of arguing, Mother laid out the guidelines for Bryan to follow. "Bryan, this has gone far enough. Either you get out and go into school, or I'll have to go in and ask Mr. Phillips to come out here and take you in himself. You don't want the principal to come after you, do you?"

"I don't care. He can't get me to go in," Bryan spoke stubbornly.

"I'll bet he can. Mr. Phillips has handled kids a lot meaner than you. If you don't get out, I'm going in after him."

Stone–faced Bryan stared out the window, refusing to respond.

"I'm also going to tell your Daddy. He'll come from work if he has to and give you a strong spanking. You don't want him to spank you, do you?"

"Daddy won't come from work. He can't get off—his boss won't let him." Bryan knew he could call his mother's bluff.

The argument went on for 15 minutes before Mother followed through with her threat to solicit cooperation from the principal. While she stood in the school office waiting for Mr. Phillips, she was surprised to see Bryan walk through the hallway and past the principal's office. Mother opened the office door and asked her son, "Where are you going? What are you doing?"

"I'm going to class, Mom. What am I supposed to be doing?"

That battle settled, Mother thought she had gotten her point across to Bryan that she would not budge on the rule of school attendance. She felt satisfied with herself for not letting her son change her mind.

Yet, the very next day, the scene from the preceding day repeated itself. Astonished that Bryan had not learned a lesson from the previous day, she found herself wondering what it would take to establish control over him. Nothing she tried seemed to be effective any longer.

Bryan's mother had provided verbal boundaries for him. It was clearly stated that it was expected that he attend school. She also told her son what she intended to do if he chose to violate the rule and even followed through with her threat. But to her chagrin, Bryan tested her authority the very next day.

Bryan had learned the previous day just how difficult it was for his mother to allow him to freely choose to make a mistake. By threatening her son, arguing with him, and reasoning with him, she had tried her hardest to make the choice for him. It was only after her effort to force Bryan to accept the stated rule had failed that she followed through with outside intervention from the principal.

Seeing that the struggle for control had ended, Bryan went into the school building. Though his mother had won the battle to get her son into school, she had lost the war for emotional control through her labored attempt to force a choice on the boy. The result was a continuation of Bryan's argumentative ways.

In order to successfully manage the oppositional child, the parent must be willing to quickly accept the first choice made by the child. To try to change his mind gives emotional control to him, prolonging the likelihood that behaviors of similar or greater intensity will be displayed in the future.

Communication with the oppositional child should be positive. The oppositional child is one who can elicit much talk from the parents. Unfortunately, much of that talk is in the form of arguing or lectures.

There is one major rule of communication that must be followed in order to have effective dialogue with the oppositional child: Avoid giving opinions, alternative points of views, constructive criticism, or advice to this child unless the child asks or is obviously ready to accept such direction from an adult. To do otherwise will simply result in a struggle for power and control.

It is common for the parent to provide the oppositional child with information which could be quite useful. But because of the child's tunnel vision, its value is not recognized. For example:

- A 16 year old could benefit from a discussion on driver safety.

- A five year old should profit from a statement about sharing.

- A 12 year old needs information about social interaction with the opposite sex.

Many children and adolescents will accept communication from a parent aimed at personal growth and improvement—but not one who is oppositional. Because of his forceful way of seeing the world through his own eyes and no others, he is determined to learn life's lessons from firsthand experience. He usually fails to realize that others in life have had more experiences than he, and they could prevent the mistakes that are inevitable.

Because the oppositional child is often frustrating to deal with, communication with him can be equally frustrating. One of the chief writers of the New Testament, the Apostle Paul, tells us, "Do not embitter your children, or they will become discouraged" (Col. 3:21). To avoid making difficult circumstances worse, communication with the oppositional child requires two critical elements that are difficult to develop: patience and proper timing. I would suggest three guidelines aimed at shaping these communication skills.

1. Demonstrate listening instead of direct intervention. The oppositional child is by nature an opinionated person. Behind any statement or behavior made by this child are numerous strong beliefs and emotions. Many of these beliefs are correct; many are incorrect. Many of the emotions are appropriate to the circumstance at hand; many are exaggerated.

The oppositional child needs to be allowed to express the full range of his beliefs and emotions as a way of relieving some of the tension built up inside him. The parent can help the oppositional child meet this need by becoming actively involved in listening to the child's full complement of thoughts. This activity will even require hearing many statements with which the parent disagrees. These statements must be accepted along with those that seem to be more sensible.

—Case Study—

Leon was furious as he came home on a Saturday afternoon. He had been playing basketball with some friends at a nearby park. His mother readily noticed his irritation.

"That's a long face, Leon. Something must have gone wrong."

"It's that stupid Larry Everson! He makes up all these dumb rules when we play anything. He doesn't even know anything about basketball. I play on a team and he thinks he knows more than I do. He doesn't know anything!"

"Larry must have taken charge of the game—told everybody what to do."

"Not only that, Mom, but he was acting like we were all younger than he is. Who does he think he is? He wanted his team to call him 'coach.' I told them they didn't have to. Then he tried to tell me to shut up. So I just hit him. I'd had all I could take, Mom!"

"You mean you and Larry were fighting? That ended the game pretty quickly, I guess." Mother disapproved of her son fighting, but recognized that the boy needed to continue to talk if she was to have any effect on him.

"Yeah, it did." Leon was becoming more subdued. "The other guys are still at the park playing. I was too mad. I knew I'd better leave before things got worse. That Larry really makes me mad!" Leon's voice began to rise again.

By this time Mother had momentarily stopped her activity. She waited until Leon spoke up again.

"I'm staying around here this afternoon. I'm not letting someone like Larry Everson boss me around. If they want me to play with them any time soon they have to come ask. And I might tell them no.'"

With that statement Leon had finished his outburst. He grumbled periodically for the next few minutes, but soon became more composed.

Leon's mother had not spoken many words but had communicated effectively with her son. She made several statements to the boy to give him confidence that she understood his viewpoint. Leon, thus, felt that he could continue to express his thoughts and emotions.

Mother avoided the temptation to tell Leon her opinion, give him advice, or scold him. She recognized that any of these responses would have presented a barrier to communication with her son. She knew that the time would present itself when Leon was not so upset. Then she could discuss with him the importance of getting along with others and ways to accomplish this goal. The goal at present was to allow Leon to express the emotions beneath his outward irritation.

As is common, Leon turned the opportunity to express himself into a chance to decide how he would solve his current dilemma. With no limits from his mother, he determined it best to avoid contact with his rival, Larry. Through his own responsible thinking, he decided what he could do to alleviate his feelings of emotional discomfort.

2. *Let your actions speak for you.* I've had many oppositional children and teenagers tell me that they know their parents' thoughts so well, they can almost speak for them. Parents of these children, however, frequently question whether or not the youngster comprehends the reasons behind the statements and disciplinary actions that are displayed by the adult. Thus, they frequently add a lecture to the punishment that must be given to the child.

My experience with oppositional children leads me to believe that these youths *do* recognize and understand their parents' stance on most issues. Their lack of agreement on many important matters does not diminish their comprehension.

Many power struggles result from the parent's desire to teach the child valuable lessons about life through discussion. My recommendation, however, is to be quick to retreat from a conversation in which it is obvious that the child will refuse to view matters from an alternate point of view. Such a dialogue will inevitably become an argument. That argument will then become an opportunity for the oppositional child to exert control over the adults. Keep in mind that this child will swiftly turn a war of words into a struggle for emotional control.

I do not advocate that the parent relinquish his role as the leader of the household. On the contrary, potential confrontations offer the chance to demonstrate positive strength.

—Case Study—

Lance had agreed that he would be home from his part-time job shortly after 3:45 P.M. with the family car. His father needed the car to run several errands late that afternoon. Neglecting his promise to his father, Lance arrived home at 5:30 P.M. He knew his father would be upset.

As Lance went into the house, he saw displeasure on his father's face. Sternly his father remarked, "Lance, you're late. I needed the car this afternoon. We had agreed that you would be home by 4 o' clock."

Lance provided an excuse for his tardiness. Dad had heard several versions of the story before. Rather than focus on Lance's limp excuse, Dad concentrated on the way his son would be held accountable for his irresponsibility.

"Tardiness of this nature is not acceptable. When I get home after going to the store, we'll discuss the consequences of your choice."

Later that evening, Lance and his father had a brief conversation about the boy's poor judgment. Dad explained that Lance would not have use of the family car for the next few days because of his lack of dependability.

Lance's father chose not to allow an incident about his son's misbehavior to become an occasion for an argument to occur. He maintained his focus on the problem at hand and did not become sidetracked by unrelated matters. He properly displayed a sense of displeasure on his face without letting the emotion become too burdensome. He called his son into accountability without stripping him of a sense of dignity.

Most importantly, Dad allowed his actions to communicate his opinion about Lance's behavior. He recognized that the provision of a negative consequence (a behavioral boundary) denoted displeasure with the youth's judgment. Further comment was not needed. Lance was assumed to have the ability to surmise that promptness with the family car was valued. Tardiness was frowned upon.

By avoiding statements that are barriers to communication, the parent is in a much greater position to assume leadership in the home. Power struggles are averted because emphasis remains on behavior. Control is maintained by the parent largely because of statements that are avoided. The child is allowed to assume what he will about the parent's beliefs and emotions. It is surprising to find how frequently his conclusions are accurate.

3. *Develop rapport before using confrontation.* It is an understatement to say that the oppositional child needs guidance. If left to his own devices, the results of this child's venture through life may be frightening. As the parent communicates with the child, he must give him timely information that will be of use in the difficult times that all children experience. Because timing is such a critical element in conveying necessary constructive criticism to the oppositional child, the parent must take precautions to develop proper rapport with the child. Rapport is best developed by demonstrating to the child a willingness to view life from his point of view. It is only after the oppositional child feels understood and

accepted by the adult that he will absorb critical statements aimed at helping the child grow emotionally.

Perhaps the most costly error to make with the oppositional child is to jump too quickly at the opportunity to correct an error in behavior or judgment. Numerous statements to the child indicating that the adult correctly perceives the child should be made prior to offering helpful advice. Helpful constructive criticism comes, then, from one who has shown a willingness to listen to alternative points of view.

While healthy communication skills are at the heart of developing rapport with the oppositional child, other efforts can bring about positive results.

There is no substitute for time spent with the oppositional child. The willingness to become submerged in the child's life for even a few moments a day creates a strong bond between the parent and child. This time can be spent talking about the day's events or engaging in a game or activity of the child's choosing. Heavy problems of the world may be entertained. The point of the individual time should not be competition, problem solving, or goal-setting. Its purpose should simply be the enjoyment of being together.

Following the democratic process in the home makes the oppositional child feel that his vote counts. A child who feels that his voice is heard will more likely cooperate than compete. In a democratic household the parents serve as leaders who maintain an interest in the needs and opinions of the child. Households run by dictatorship are susceptible to uprisings by argumentative children bent on taking over the position of power within the family.

Physical touch is important to the establishment of rapport. Physical contact with a parent can mean many things to the child or adolescent. It can provide a sense of security in the knowledge that someone bigger and more experienced at life is present. Touch can convey feelings of affection and emotional warmth. Respect can be communicated nonverbally by a simple nudge, pat, hug, or handshake. The parent can display his willingness to enter the child's world of experience through touch. In short, the parent who will come physically close to the oppositional child encourages a positive attachment with that child.

Because the oppositional child in many ways forces the parent to focus his attention on disciplinary matters, the need for a solid relationship of mutual trust and respect can become lost in the shuffle. Yet without a positive rapport with the child or teen-ager, efforts at managing argumentative behavior will meet with mediocre results at best. A healthy relationship greatly narrows communication gaps between parent and child.

Summary

The oppositional child may be characterized by a distinguishable set of traits. The oppositional child generally has qualities of each of these five primary characteristics.

- The authority of adults is routinely challenged by the oppositional child in his quest for control.

- Negative behavior is displayed even though it may serve no purpose.

- The child thrives on the excitement of competition with others, especially adults.

- Behavior is considered by this child to be wrong if punishment follows. It is deemed okay if nothing negative happens.

- Normal discipline measures seem to be ineffective.

There is not a single identifiable cause for oppositional behavior. This pattern of behavior develops as a result of several factors:

- Some children are more difficult to control because of their own inborn tendency to be that way.

- Whether intended or not, adults may reinforce the likelihood that a child will continue to be oppositional by reactions given to the child.

- Negative behavior styles may be presented to the child in the form of parental role models.

- A child may act in oppositional ways because his need to communicate inner thoughts and emotions is not adequately satisfied.

An understanding of the dynamics of the power struggle is essential to understanding the ways of the oppositional child. A power struggle develops when (*a*) a behavior problem presents itself, (*b*) the parent takes responsibility to solve the problem, (*c*) the child searches for a potential reward, and (*d*) the struggle shifts to one of emotional control.

Power struggles serve little constructive purpose to either the child or the parent. The child is encouraged to continue to act in negative ways, while the adult senses a loss of control and a feeling of despair.

Managing oppositional behavior requires more than a search for a more effective discipline weapon. Several equally important guidelines must be followed in managing the oppositional child.

- The parent must maintain control of his emotions by keeping a healthy detachment from the child's oppositional behavior.

- The consistent enforcement of behavioral boundaries allows the child to be responsible for himself.

- Effective communication with the oppositional child frees the child from the need to more forcefully express his emotions. The child who feels understood is more likely to choose cooperation over competition.

Study Session 1

Objective:

To identify oppositional behavior patterns of your child and determine how you, as a parent, react to those behaviors.

Biblical Reference: Luke 15:11–24

The Parable of the Prodigal Son is an example of the difficulties an oppositional child may experience as a result of his lack of judgment. The loving father knew his son had to learn from his own experiences before he would accept the father's guidance.

Discussion Questions:

1. What are the typical ways your child displays oppositional behavior? Is there a predictable pattern to his behavior?

2. What effect does your effort to discipline have on this oppositional child? Does discipline only seem to make him more argumentative? In what way could your child actually gain an advantage over you as you try to display leadership over him?

3. When your child becomes difficult to deal with, how do you react to him? With anger? Frustration? Indecisiveness? Bewilderment? How does your child interpret your reaction to him?

4. Are there ways that you display oppositional behavior patterns that could be imitated by your child?

5. What messages is your child trying to communicate through his negative behavior? Even if you disagree with your child, do you understand his point of view?

Assignments:

1. Work on being an active observer of the interactions you have with your oppositional child. Give special attention to how positive you are in your communication with him. If needed, be more attentive to him as you speak to one another.

2. Make a point to take your child on an outing this week. Take him out for a hamburger, a movie of his choice, or to a park to play. Don't take anyone else along with you.

Study Session 2

Objective:

To develop a strategy for providing effective leadership to your oppositional child.

Biblical Reference: Prov. 13:3; Eph. 4:26

Note that while discipline is an identified need of a child, it is most effective when the parent has proper control over his own emotions. Reflect on how the emotional control of the parent places the burden of behavioral responsibility squarely on the young person.

Discussion Questions:

1. What reaction would you receive from your oppositional child if you showed a willingness to listen to his complaints rather than trying to out–argue him?

2. Does your child know your opinions on most issues related to his behavior? Does he know what you expect of him? Do you find yourself preaching the same messages over and over to him anyway? How does your child take advantage of your desire to teach him a lesson?

3. In what ways does your child succeed in creating a lack of unity between you and other authority figures in his life (your spouse, other relatives, teachers and principals, etc.)? How does a lack of consistency among authority figures contribute to continual oppositional behavior?

4. How often do you reward your child through a positive comment, extra privilege, or tangible item? Conversely, how often do you find yourself punishing him? How does your child interpret the disciplinary approach you use?

Assignments:

1. Make an effort to increase your positive interaction with your oppositional child. In addition to offering more verbal praise, demonstrate that you have listened to him by commenting on

his viewpoints and asking him to tell you more about how he sees things.

2. Talk this week with others who are in a position of authority over your child. Let them know you are supportive of them. Determine among yourselves to work together for the good of your child.

2

The Silent Explosion—

The Sensitive Child

—*Case Study*—

AT AGE 21, SHERRY RECOUNTED her life's history for me. She had been referred to my office by her parents, Mr. and Mrs. Wilkins, who expressed concern that over the past three or four years their daughter had experienced something of a change in her personality. Uncharacteristically, she had become argumentative and difficult to talk to. Her emotions always seemed to be on edge. Whereas the Sherry of old was docile and gentle, the "new" Sherry was more bold and aggressive. Arguments between Sherry and her close friends and family members were now far more common than in previous years. In fact, Mrs. Wilkins remarked that she had been in more disagreements with her daughter in the past four years than in all the previous 17 years combined.

Sherry was talkative and quite willing to discuss her current relationship difficulties. She viewed her personality pattern as more stable than did her family members. She rejected the theory that she may have undergone a major shift in personal characteristics. She did admit that her style of relating to others had changed. Rather than passively respond to others, she had become more assertive, and even aggressive. Her moods seemed to change more rapidly than before. She had always been sensitive to how others perceived her, but now it seemed that she became upset over trivial matters.

Sherry agreed that her way of managing relationships was not healthy. She purposely had become more bold and outspoken, but recognized that her efforts had not been fruitful. She did not want to remain passive and withdrawn as she had been in earlier years. That tack had caused her much loneliness. She wanted help understanding herself, but did not know where to begin.

Defining the Sensitive Child

The sensitive child poses a unique problem to parents because his behavior is not like that of a child who is more outwardly disobedient. Like Sherry, the sensitive child may not display significant behavioral problems until adolescence. Previously compliant and easily managed, he becomes resentful, rebellious, and deceitful. He usually behaves as he does out of his own deep emotional response to others. Although resistance to authority is certainly evident, negative expressions are exhibited not primarily as a means of controlling others, but to signal the need for deeper understanding from others.

Unlike the oppositional child, the sensitive child does not enjoy conflict. He much prefers being cooperative rather than competitive. When offered the opportunity, this child will talk freely about emotions and feelings, shunning the idea that openness is to be avoided.

Sensitive children display a wide range of emotions. Not all follow an identical pattern of emotional expression, but many will exhibit numerous common traits. The more common are as follows.

Awareness of how others view him is keen. Probably more than other children, the sensitive child notices the way others react to him. Little escapes his attention. He notices subtle facial expressions or changes in the tone of a voice. He tends to interpret words and actions more strongly than is intended by others. He is overly self-conscious and relies heavily on others' opinions of him as he develops his sense of self–worth. Yet, because he overanalyzes the messages sent to him by others, he develops an unhealthy sense of value about himself. He responds to the world with a faulty idea of how others actually perceive him.

—Case Study—

Warren's family could be described as normal in most respects. Though both parents held full–time jobs, they tried to spend as much time with their children as their busy schedules allowed. They were not harsh in their discipline, but provided firm boundaries within which their children were expected to behave. They did their best to communicate openly with one another.

Warren's two sisters presented their parents with few worries, but Warren failed to respond in the same manner. He was frequently upset because of words a family member had spoken to him. He tended to take a simple statement and make it more complex than seemed necessary. He whined and cried more than anyone in the family. If anyone in the family worried about something, it was Warren.

Despite the family's efforts to build positive self–esteem in Warren, he complained of feeling less capable than others. He seemed to feel that he was all alone in the world. He demanded more attention than his sisters. There was little the family could say to cause him to feel more positively about himself.

Like Warren, many sensitive children have an intensity that makes them difficult to understand. They do not approach life in a relaxed manner. They tend to take life more seriously than perhaps they should. Trivial matters are frequently blown out of proportion.

I have known parents who feel they are constantly walking on eggshells around their sensitive children. Just when it seems that the child's life is running smoothly, he will misinterpret something said or done by another person and is off again on another of his emotional roller coaster rides.

The tendency of the sensitive child to be overly self–conscious of how others view him is an example of how a good characteristic can become imbalanced. It is a potential strength for an individual to be perceptive of his environment. Yet, too often this type of child will take a grain of truth and blow it out of proportion.

Emotions are not properly asserted. Even though the emotional river runs deep through the soul of the sensitive child, the expression of those emotions frequently is not done in a healthy way. Young children of this type tend to manage their own emotions by withholding them from others. Adolescents may become more volatile in their emotional expression, having learned that withholding emotions too commonly results in depressed feelings.

A common pattern for these children is that as they become older, their emotional expressions become more pronounced. Rather than view this change as a shift in personality, I view it as the adolescent's attempt to unleash the emotional discomfort that has been building for numerous years. This shift in expression represents the child's effort to find internal peace, but it fails to soothe him.

Typical inappropriate expressions of the young child include:

- Not talking to others, even when the opportunity is appropriate.

- Procrastinating in order to avoid confrontation.

- Waiting for others to approach him with an offer of help.

- Pretending to feel emotional comfort even though his internal hurt is intense.

- Developing physical conditions or complaints without a medical basis (e.g., wetting or soiling clothes, stomachaches, headaches).

Typical inappropriate expressions of the older child or adolescent include:

- Accusations about how others feel (e.g., "You never listen to me;" "You never do what I want;" or "You always look at me like that.").

- Unrealistic expectations of others.

- Uncharacteristically strong emotional outbursts.

- Obvious signs of dissatisfaction or even depression.

- Rejection of attempts by others to be reinforcing or encouraging.

- An unforgiving attitude toward those who have erred in even a slight way; holds grudges.

I should point out that though it is common for a sensitive child to become more outwardly expressive of his emotional discomfort as he grows older, he is usually selective in revealing his feelings. Family, friends, or other acquaintances of the child may be surprised to learn of the hostile tendencies this person has developed through the years. In general, the sensitive child unleashes his emotions when around family members, but remains relatively unassertive with others.

The tendency to depend on others is strong. Early in life the sensitive child looks to others to provide a sense of security. The young toddler may be called a "mother's child." He feels uncomfortable being alone and will resist any circumstance that creates a feeling of internal isolation. Most children adjust to separation from their parents, but the sensitive child struggles over this matter.

Many children with sensitive inclinations move through life with relatively few adjustment problems. They surround themselves with a small group of close friends. Primary responsibilities are carried out in an obliging manner. They are frequently liked by adults who recognize them as mature and reliable.

Yet, other children in this category fail to make a positive adjustment to their own temperament. Being dependent on others, they actually "invite" parents to be overly protective of them. Acting in a helpless manner, the child avoids having to function on his own (see figure 5). He requires almost constant attention, but rather than gain this attention from others by behaving badly, he does it by being submissive.

Many sensitive children are described as being easy to raise as infants and toddlers. Parents report receiving great enjoyment with the child because of the ease with which the youngster follows instructions and directions. Problems develop, however, when parents want the child to show greater independence, but the child resists.

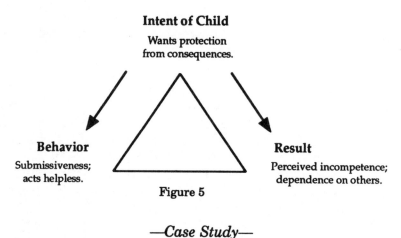

Intent of Child

Wants protection
from consequences.

Behavior

Submissiveness;
acts helpless.

Result

Perceived incompetence;
dependence on others.

Figure 5

—Case Study—

At age 17, Janet's friends seemed to live only for the weekend. Friday and Saturday nights meant opportunities for social gatherings. The talk at school often centered around plans for the weekend.

Yet, Janet avoided inclusion in these normal teen activities. Occasionally she would go out with a friend but almost always came in earlier than other teenagers. Janet was easily upset by her parents' encouragement to be more socially active. She complained that her parents placed too much pressure on her to do what she did not want to do. Because she felt misunderstood by her family, Janet became reclusive. Periodically, however, she had bursts of emotion that revealed the strength of feeling hidden within her.

It was Janet's lack of adjustment to her own temperament that created many of her inner feelings of isolation. Though in many respects an easy teenager to manage (she was rarely involved in "troubled" behavior), her sensitive nature rendered her helpless in comparison to other teens who were more socially active and assertive. As a defense against her obvious differences from others, she chose to cling to a life–style that was safe. Yet her unwillingness to become independent created a sensation of internal unrest.

While many interpret the overly submissive behavior of the sensitive child as a sign of maturity, parents of this type of child are often concerned that he is too compliant. To be sure, there is a pleasant appearance of responsibility attached to this young person's behavior. Yet, the lack of emotional independence can signal the potential for the unhappiness that is often associated with an overdependence on others.

Self-esteem is fragile. Because he views the responses of others in an overly critical manner, the sensitive child is prone to downplay his own sense of importance as well. A vicious negative cycle may evolve. Certain events encourage self-doubt which in turn increases the probability that future events will also be viewed negatively. The result can be a child with a penchant toward viewing himself negatively even when circumstances do not warrant it. Some examples are:

- A 15-year-old girl who is turned down by a boy with a poor reputation surmises that if a "nobody" rejects her, she is certainly not worthy of a boyfriend with a more positive reputation.

- A seven-year-old boy clings to his parent while other children are playing. Efforts by his playmates to coax him to join in the fun are seen by the boy as an unwanted possibility for social rejection.

- A 16-year-old high school student believes that her geometry teacher is intentionally putting her on the spot by requiring that she solve a difficult problem on the chalkboard before her classmates.

- A 10-year-old boy openly talks negatively about himself when he hears his parents disagree over whether he should be allowed to sign up for Little League baseball.

All children develop their self-esteem as a result of the interactions they have with others. Because of his tentative nature, the sensitive child may create situations that lead him to erroneously conclude that his worth as a person is in some way diminished. As seen in the examples above, he may choose to maintain a safe distance between himself and perceived emotional risk. Or, he may develop opinions of himself that are based on faulty assumptions rather than the reality of the actual circumstance. In a paradoxical twist of events, the thoughts and behavior of the sensitive child prompt a reaction from others that encourages the very emotional discomfort he so desperately wishes to avoid.

Discomfort is displayed through socially unaccepted behavior. Because the overly sensitive child is prone to hide emotions, he frequently expresses feelings of internal discomfort through behavior. Many parents discount unacceptable behavior as an inappropriate way for the child to gain attention. While it is certainly true that misbehavior can signal a desire for attention, it is wise to look beneath the surface of the behavior see if the stronger emotional needs are being expressed.

Some ways a child may disguise emotional discomfort are seen in the examples given below:

- A 14–year–old daughter shouts and even swears at her parents when they express disapproval of her choice of boyfriends.

- Whining and clinging to mother are demonstrated by a three–year–old child who does not wish to interact with other children.

- A nine–year–old boy adamantly refuses to attend school by claiming illness. His physician maintains that nothing is medically wrong with the child.

- Preoccupation with neatness and orderliness grows into compulsive rituals for a 12–year–old girl.

In each of these examples a child has an emotional need that is an outgrowth of his own sensitive nature. Yet, rather than openly acknowledge the emotions deep within, the child displays feelings through unacceptable behavior. Indeed, the child may not be capable of labeling his own emotions. He can only hope that an astute parent reads between the lines of his words and actions to correctly identify the hurt he feels within. It is only then that he can begin to hope that relief is on its way.

Factors Influencing the Sensitive Child's Behavior

An inborn disposition toward sensitivity may be present. In the same way that a child may be born with a penchant toward difficult-to-manage behavior, sensitive behavior may also have its roots in the inborn temperament of a child. One of the greatest barriers many parents face in dealing with the problems of their children is their own guilt. Too many parents assume all responsibility for their child's behavior, ignoring the fact that a child comes into the world with his own emotional agenda.

We would do well as parents to recognize that children cannot change their basic personality structures. To endorse such a thought can allow a parent to relinquish the urge to mold the child into the shape that parent desires him to be. Certainly the child's personality is colored by his experiences, but its basic expression is first seen during the early weeks and months of life.

My experience with sensitive children has led me to conclude that several key behavioral trends are commonly displayed as a result of this child's inborn nature. An understanding of these trends helps the parent identify his role in shaping or refining the child's basic personality style. I touched on many of these trends while defining the sensitive child, but will enumerate them again.

A primary desire of this child is to fit in with others. Although not always successful in his efforts, the sensitive child is keenly aware of his relationships. It is not necessary that this child have a wide range of friends, but it is important for him to have at least a few people with whom he feels a close emotional tie.

The self-esteem of the sensitive child is more fragile. Because he so strongly desires close personal relationships, he does not always correctly evaluate the responses others have toward him. His tendency to overinterpret what others say causes him to absorb feedback that is faulty. The self-image he develops is thus shaped by his own tendency to be critical of the words and actions of others.

More time and energy from parents is required by the sensitive child than most other children. I know of a family who has a daughter in this category. When the child was very young, the father became aware of her demands for a great deal of attention. He recognized that this was an indicator of the large amount of time and energy he and his wife would be required to provide if they hoped to fulfill their desire to see their daughter develop into a healthy adult.

His early hunch proved to be correct as this daughter cherished the abundant attention that was made available to her throughout the years. Her personality "blueprint" seemed to require more individual focus than did that of her two siblings.

There are few indifferent feelings in the sensitive child. Emotions are not expressed simply to release tension. There is virtually always a message beneath his behavior. This child wants to communicate and dearly wants to feel understood. Because he is a "feeling–oriented" person, relationships are important.

Reinforcement of overly sensitive behavior can increase its frequency. It is not negative to be sensitive. The sensitive child has many positive behavioral traits. Yet, as is true with any behavioral characteristic, sensitivity can develop into a pattern that has potentially harmful effects.

I believe that the sensitive child is one of the most difficult children to manage simply because of the child's own tender nature. It is difficult for most parents to be harsh toward this kind of child. In fact, most parents of sensitive children will readily admit that they sometimes melt emotionally because the child's personality is so "soft."

The inclination of parents to be less assertive with the sensitive child contributes to the development of the negative elements of what is otherwise a pleasant temperament. Through the course of time, the child learns that his sensitivity causes him to be seen by others as special. He takes advantage of opportunities to use his disposition to his advantage. The predictable sympathetic response from a caring and well–meaning parent encourages the child to continue to act in inappropriate ways. It is possible for the child to become helpless after years of exchanges with others in which his sensitive nature is essentially rewarded.

—Case Study—

William and his mother had been emotionally close since the time William was born. He was responsive to his mother's loving gestures during his infancy and toddler years. As he grew older, Mother found herself providing William with frequent small favors. It was easy to be lenient with him because he was such an emotionally receptive child.

As an example, one house rule was that each child had to eat all the food on his plate at mealtime. William learned, however, that the rule was often broken for him. He discovered that with a little nudging he could get his mother to help him complete his assigned chores. And experience also taught him that his mother would come to his rescue any time he faced a conflict or problem with his friends.

By the time William reached early adolescence, his behavior had begun to change for the worse. In my office, his mother stated with exasperation that she could not understand William's shift toward rebellion. She was hurt because her son did not seem to appreciate the attention and sacrifices that had been made for him during his childhood. She grieved that her once caring son had become insensitive and hard to manage. She could not comprehend the anger she now received from her son.

William had not lost his personality. He was still the same emotion-laden person he had been as a younger child. Yet, experience had taught him to use his inborn nature in an essentially negative manner. Through the consistent responses made toward him he had learned that his sensitive nature could be used in his favor to avoid responsibility. He learned that laziness was allowed. As an adolescent, he openly challenged anyone, even his mother, who attempted to take away the "rewards" he had been given through the years as a result of his sensitive character (see figure 6).

Unreasonable expectations may create a danger. Parents can unknowingly contribute to the frustration hidden beneath the child's misbehavior. It is easy for the parent to fall into the trap of establishing a child's goals and expectations based on parental desire rather than the child's own desires and capabilities.

Children react to pressure in a variety of ways. A competitive and aggressive child may respond with enthusiasm to the opportunity to reach a goal that has been placed before him. The sensitive child, however, may have a negative reaction to expectations that did not originate within himself.

—Case Study—

As a junior high school athlete, Mark showed promise as a track runner. Since he had never before been involved in competitive activities, Mark's venture into an organized athletic program was a new experience to his family. Surprised by his newly discovered talent, Mark felt he had found a way to make a name for himself over the next few years.

Mark's dad was also pleasantly surprised at his son's running ability and took a strong interest in the youth's progress. In the past, he had been frustrated by Mark's lack of interest in any activity that could potentially provide a boost in the boy's relatively weak self-esteem. His athletic success could offer the outlet for personal accomplishment Mark had previously lacked.

Hoping to encourage Mark to higher levels of success, Dad became heavily involved in Mark's running program. When possible, Dad slipped away from the office to watch the team's workout. He talked regularly with the track coach in order to stay abreast of Mark's progress. Of course, Dad attended all of Mark's track meets. It seemed that his own nervous anticipation of Mark's races was stronger than what Mark himself experienced.

For a couple of years, Mark enjoyed his dad's high level of interest in his athletic ventures. The father and son had never shared a common experience such as the one provided by Mark's running. As they talked regularly about Mark's abilities and progress, Mark's self-confidence soared.

By the time Mark reached the 10th grade, he began to sense that his dad was losing perspective of their shared interest. Rather than interpret his dad's presence at workouts and track meets as a gesture of support, Mark felt pressured to perform at continually higher levels. What once had been a source of enjoyment for Mark now brought tension and internal frustration.

Not wanting to disappoint his father, Mark continued to go through the paces of his daily workout schedule. Yet, his behavior toward others changed, and he lost his enthusiasm for the sport. After a bad workout, he became sullen and would often pout. Mark's dad tried to talk to him about his negative moods, explaining that he would not continue his athletic progress unless his attitude improved. Despite his dad's efforts to instill a renewed sense of emotional control in him, Mark's downward spiral continued. Not wishing to confront his father, Mark kept his thoughts to himself.

A large contributing factor to Mark's emotional deterioration was the presence of expectations that did not match his ability to cope. Because Mark's temperament did not predispose him to be aggressive and competitive, the increasing wave of high expectations created frustration in him.

A realistic goal for Mark would have been to allow him to participate in track activities as an opportunity for athletic expression and social approval. To impose higher expectations on him was more than his potentially fragile personality would allow. The result of a mismatch between parental expectations and a child's emotional makeup can lead to negative feelings and behaviors on the part of that child.

Communication voids with the sensitive child may intensify his emotions. I have met only a few sensitive children and teenagers who had difficulty communicating their emotions with others. It is true that many are slow to trust another person to the point where

Parent's Behavior	Child's Interpretation
loving gestures . . .	. . . *Mother loves me.*
lenience . . .	. . . *Mother makes exceptions for me.*
rescue from conflicts . . .	. . . *Mother will take my problems as her own.*
makes repeated sacrifices . . .	. . . *I can take advantage of Mother.*
demands responsibility . . .	. . . *Mother will give in to my defiance.*

A sensitive child can invite a parent to be protective of him. The result can be unexpected rebellion.

Figure 6

talking becomes easy, but virtually all will eventually talk openly with people whom they perceive as openminded and willing to listen.

I find that sensitive children have deep convictions about their own feelings and beliefs. Their emotional responsiveness to others is different than that of the oppositional child. Whereas the latter child's intent is often to gain control over the authority associated with the parent, the sensitive child desires communication that will result in mutual understanding between himself and the parent.

There are several communication stumbling blocks that seem to be especially harmful to relationship development with an overly sensitive child. Three common barriers to communication are as follows:

Barrier #1

Offering a solution to a problem as soon as the problem presents itself often offends the overly sensitive child. Because of his tendency to consider the depth of problems more seriously than others, the sensitive child or adolescent is prone to initially react to a problem with emotions rather than with a rational line of thought. Thus, to become overly analytical of a problem before the child has experienced the full range of his own emotions may encourage further discomfort.

A sensitive 16 year old who has just been turned down for a date will feel further hurt if his parent expresses a simple analysis such as, "Maybe she turned you down because she hasn't gotten over breaking up with her last boyfriend." The parent's perception may be correct, but since the verbal response does not match the teenager's need to discuss his feeling of rejection, the likelihood of a negative reaction from the son has been increased.

Barrier #2

Putting an overly sensitive child in the position of having to defend himself pushes him to rebellion. Related to the sensitive child's tendency to reject a solution that is too quickly offered is an equal inclination to bristle when constructive criticism is offered too quickly. Feeling the need to protect his own emotions, he will likely express what seems to be an unnecessary strong reaction. A sensitive child who has been told too quickly that the number of confrontations he has with a neighborhood rival will decrease if he will learn to use proper manners may respond, "Why don't you ever listen to me? You always believe what everybody else tells you!" A teenager who has been told that her poor eating habits will make her look fat may burst into tears claiming that everyone thinks she is ugly.

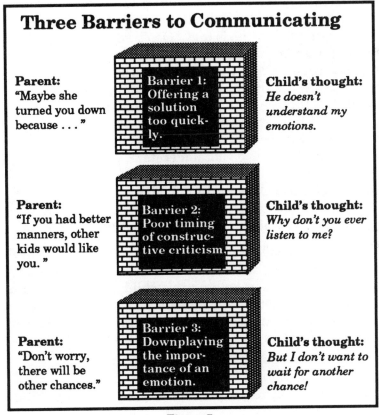

Three Barriers to Communicating

Parent:
"Maybe she turned you down because ... "

Barrier 1: Offering a solution too quickly.

Child's thought:
He doesn't understand my emotions.

Parent:
"If you had better manners, other kids would like you."

Barrier 2: Poor timing of constructive criticism.

Child's thought:
Why don't you ever listen to me?

Parent:
"Don't worry, there will be other chances."

Barrier 3: Downplaying the importance of an emotion.

Child's thought:
But I don't want to wait for another chance!

Figure 7

A frequent barrier to communicating with the sensitive child is a parent's tendency to provide the child with too much information, advice, or opinions. Though the words being stated may have merit, they are transformed into poison when absorbed by a child whose emotional state causes him to be unprepared for such frank dialogue.

Barrier #3

Efforts to lessen the blow caused by a disappointing circumstance leave the overly sensitive child feeling all alone with his problem. A common barrier to communicating with the sensitive child lies in the misbelief that the child can be readily talked out of an emotional reaction by having him believe that the problem at hand is really not as serious as he seems to think.

A third grader who is told, "Don't worry; there will be other plays" after learning that he did not get an assigned part in a class play, will learn to believe that his parents do not trust his sincerity when he expresses disappointment. Feeling a lack of trust, the probability of future outbursts has increased.

To tell a 10–year–old girl, "You shouldn't feel so upset" when she has just been teased by a group of friends, leaves her feeling that her parents do not understand what it means to be the focus of a joke. To make her feelings more clearly evident in the future, she will use more forceful means.

Managing the Sensitive Child

It is not possible (nor even desirable) to create a different personality in a sensitive child. There are, however, several feasible goals to work toward in helping this child accept his own nature and express his emotions in a healthy way. The parent has influence over several areas of the child's emotional and behavioral development that are particularly applicable to the sensitive child. These include:

- Developing a stronger sense of self–worth in the child.

- Teaching the child to be independent and competent rather than dependent on others.

- Improving the child's skills in coping with frustrating experiences or even failure.

- Creating opportunities to promote better communication skills within the child.

There is a tendency for the parent of a sensitive child to relax the demands that might otherwise be placed on that child simply because he is emotionally soft. The wisdom found in the Proverbs reminds the parent, "Do not withhold discipline from a child" (Prov. 23:13). The recognition that the sensitive child needs active guidance to prevent his sensitivity from becoming an emotional liability can help the parent be more assertive in family management.

The following guidelines address what I believe to be the most important focal points when redirecting the behavior of the overly sensitive child.

Choose which behaviors will receive attention. Through the course of time, the sensitive child has learned which of his own behaviors will evoke certain responses. Children and adolescents do not act in a completely random manner. Through careful observation of others, they learn that benefits are attached to their behavior. Unfortunately some of the benefits are not healthy for them in the long run.

For example, it is not healthy for the child to avoid meaningful contact with others out of a fear of rejection, but the immediate benefit is the avoidance of emotional discomfort. The damage comes when the child fails to learn how to confront difficult situations since life demands a certain amount of emotional discomfort.

As difficult as it may be, sensitive children must face uneasy circumstances alone. The parent must refrain from rescuing the child from potential peril.

—Case Study—

The Cochrans had two children—Christi, age 10, and Roger, age 8. Christi was a particularly sensitive child who easily took offense at any negative behavior directed toward her. She was normally a compliant child, but she had a tendency to make the most of her age advantage over her younger brother.

Like other brothers and sisters, Christi and Roger had a normal sibling rivalry. Most of their disagreements tended to be over petty matters such as territorial rights. Christi would scream at Roger for being in her bedroom without permission. She would whine and cry if Roger rode her bicycle, even though she may have just gotten off his bike.

The Cochrans were not overly concerned about their children's sibling rivalry for they recognized those minor disputes as being normal. Their concern was for the reaction they drew from Christi whenever it was necessary to correct her for her part in an argument.

In my office, the Cochrans explained that Christi would typically cry and then withdraw from the family following a mild scolding. They knew it would be wrong of them to ignore Christi's emotional outbursts altogether, for they felt Christi could learn from the negative experience of being corrected. Every effort was made to consider Christi's emotional needs by not being too harsh with her.

Further discussion of Christi's behavior revealed that out of concern for their daughter, one or both parents gave Christi special attention soon after she was corrected. Their care included such things as stroking her hair as they talked about the inappropriateness of her actions, offering a drink to her to help stop the crying, or substituting an object or activity with which Christi could become involved.

The desire of the Cochrans was to help their daughter more boldly face the criticism and instruction that she required. Our first step in treating this behavior was to identify in concrete terms the way Christi responded to correction. She cried, pouted, pushed out her lower lip, and displayed a pitiable expression on her face. Her entire expression proclaimed, "I am too sensitive. Somebody please rescue me!"

At that point, the Cochrans recognized their role in the development of Christi's behavior. By focusing on Christi's negative reaction to corrective measures, they were unwittingly encouraging further displays of hypersensitivity.

The Cochrans needed to ignore Christi's pouting and withdrawal. I explained to the Cochrans that their lack of attention might cause their daughter to become even more emotional during the initial stages of their new plan. Such a reaction would represent Christi's desire for the kind of attention to which she had grown accustomed.

To help offset Christi's reaction, she was informed by her parents of their intent to remove themselves from her presence when she became upset because of their response to her. By explaining their plan to Christi, the Cochrans lessened the feeling of abandonment Christi might momentarily experience.

To round out the plan, the Cochrans were instructed to provide verbal approval to Christi whenever she showed an increased ability to demonstrate emotional control. So, in addition to removing the undesired behavioral response, Christi was taught more appropriate behaviors. The Cochrans' efforts helped Christi to gain more control over her high level of sensitivity.

Refrain from assuming responsibility for the child's actions. I find that most sensitive children are quick to learn how to make their way into the heart of those who are close to them, especially parents. A woeful facial expression, heavy sigh, or a worried tone of voice may cause a parent to feel concern. It is understandable that parents often succumb to a child's unspoken request in their efforts to be overly protective. Most parents cannot bear the feelings of guilt that come upon them when it is necessary to take action that causes the child to feel uncomfortable.

A primary obstacle that prevents many sensitive children from experiencing happiness and self–confidence is the child's hesitance to purposely take the risks necessary to learn valuable lessons about the need to be independent. Therefore, the parent must grasp a view of the long range needs of the child. The parent must be willing to act on behalf of the child's extended emotional needs rather than attend to the immediate concerns for which the child demands prompt relief.

Examine the following list of behaviors or thoughts commonly associated with parents who become too involved in the responsibilities of their child:

- Makes decisions for the child that the child is capable of making.

- Forces resolutions on the child (e.g. "Of course you want to go bowling. It's lots of fun.").

- Is constantly occupied with the child.
- Becomes too emotionally involved in the child's choice of behaviors.
- Hates to see the child hurt as the result of a mistake.
- Has limited confidence in the child's choice of behaviors.
- Provides the child a range of options that is too limited.
- Worries constantly when the child is away from home.
- Views the child as inferior to others rather than equal.

As difficult as it may be for the parent of the sensitive child, it is important that the parent recognize that one of his primary roles is to provide childhood guidance that will result in the development of responsible behavior in the child.

I have talked with many parents whose sincere intent on raising their children according to sound spiritual principles led them to accept a passive stance as a parent. Their purpose was to display the patience and love seen in the character of God. Yet Old Testament history is fraught with illustrations of how God's love is exemplified by an active disciplinary reaction to his wayward children. This Fatherly direction helped the children of God avoid pitfalls that could have resulted in emotional harm.

I can recall from my own childhood days times that I was certain that my mother and father had erred in their management of a problem in which I was involved. At the time I did not have the wisdom that evolves through maturity to make decisions that were in my own best interest. It was the duty of my parents to allow me to feel momentary discomfort so I would be more likely to develop into an adult who had profited from these experiences.

Following are behaviors or thoughts commonly associated with parents who recognize the child's need to be responsible for his own actions:

- Recognizes the child's need to learn from his own mistakes.
- Listens to the child's point of view, even when it differs from the parent's views.

- Encourages the child to explore his own world with a sense of curiosity.

- Demonstrates belief in the democratic process.

- Maintains a healthy sense of objectivity toward the child.

- Perceives parent and child to be equal in value, even though their family roles are different.

- Influences the child by providing a positive role model.

- Seeks to stimulate the child rather than exert force.

The parent whose emphasis is placed on allowing the child to be responsible to himself differs in one major way from the parent who assumes too much liability for the child. The first parent recognizes that he can be responsible only to himself. With that recognition, he focuses on his own behavior and not upon the behavior he wants to force upon the child. He realizes that his role as parent is to provide an atmosphere that will encourage the child to learn to live within the boundaries of his own personality characteristics.

—Case Study—

Carla was the youngest of four children in her family. Her three older siblings were grown and living away from home. Being the youngest child in the family by several years, she was looked upon as unique. Her parents referred to her as their "package from heaven" since she arrived relatively late in their lives.

Carla's parents and her older siblings found her to be delightful as a young child. She seldom misbehaved and constantly did her best to please others. It seemed that she would become the shining star in the family.

When Carla reached the sixth grade in school, her life began to deteriorate. At times she seemed to be "herself," but at other times it seemed as if she had changed personalities.

Carla's parents, Mr. and Mrs. Wilkins, explained to me that their daughter had developed a habit of greatly exaggerating the truth. For example, one day she fell and skinned her knee at school. When allowed to call home to inform her mother, she embellished the incident to the point that Mrs. Wilkins feared she had been badly hurt.

Carla's eating pattern had deteriorated to the point that she seldom ate a healthy meal. She had become a rather sickly child and commonly complained of a headache, stomachache, cold, or sore throat. Because of her frequent physical complaints, she had begun sleeping in her parents' bed because that seemed to be the only way she could get a restful night of sleep.

During my first interview with Carla, I was immediately aware of her excessive sensitivity toward me. She was more cooperative than most children her age. She quickly expressed her gratitude toward me for helping her family and indicated a willingness to follow any instructions I might give her. She explained that she would do anything to get her emotions under control and bring order back to her family.

Further examination of Carla found her to be a child with classical symptoms of the sensitive child "syndrome." She was overly conscious of the way others viewed her. She withheld her emotions rather than expressing them in a candid fashion. Her identity as a person depended too much on others. She saw herself in a positive light only to the degree that others approved of her every action. She was prone to feelings of depression because of her tendency toward self–criticism.

In subsequent counseling sessions with Carla and her parents, emphasis was given to Carla's need to assume responsibility for herself. Previously Carla's parents had tried to help her by making her problems their own. They had innocently been drawn into patterns of overprotection, inhibiting Carla's ability to manage her own emotions and behaviors.

At first Carla resisted her parents' efforts to encourage her to be responsible to herself. For a period of time she showed an increase in her displays of helplessness. Mr. and Mrs. Wilkins correctly recognized the reaction as a natural response to a life–style to which she was unaccustomed. Over the course of several months, they saw their daughter develop a stronger sense of competence. She moved away from her previous need to depend solely on others to guide her through life's uncertainties and developed confidence in her own ability to handle the stresses of daily life.

Listening to the sensitive child provides emotional relief. I find sensitive children and teenagers to be one of the most accessible groups of youth in terms of communication. Because of their ready desire to please others, they tend to be more honest in revealing themselves. When the communication process is begun with a sensitive child, there is often an initial period of time in which the child withholds emotions. After the establishment of a sense of trust, however, emotions seem to pour out of this child.

As with any child, a healthy pattern of communication between the parent and sensitive child begins with the act of listening to the child. Some of the ways a child benefits from being in the presence of a listening parent include the following:

- The intensity of emotions is decreased to a level more tolerable in the child.

- A sense of respect for the child's point of view is conveyed.

- The opportunity to express a wider range of feelings is available to the child.

- The child senses that he is not all alone with his thoughts.

- Feelings of guilt are avoided because the child does not feel as if he is hiding information.

- The parents' acceptance of the child's viewpoint encourages the child to accept himself.

- "Mixed up" feelings are more neatly organized by the child.

As simple as it may seem to be, the act of listening to a child is an elusive skill. In most conversations between a parent and child, the parent hears the child's words, but may fail to fully comprehend the meaning behind those words. I like to refer to hearing as a more physical act. Listening, on the other hand, is a much more complex action. Not only must the parent hear the words of the child, but he must try to interpret those words correctly. Factors which affect he correct interpretation of words spoken by the child include:

- the child's personality

- the context of the statement
- previous events that contributed to the child's present situation
- the emotional state of the child
- the child's age and maturity level

For a parent to effectively help the sensitive child, comments made by the child should be interpreted from the child's point of view. Even though the parent may be able to recognize the flaws in the statements made by the child, the child needs to know that his point of view is taken seriously. It is at that point that the child will be more capable of receiving the wise counsel available to him from his parent.

—Case Study—

A 14–year–old girl, Lucie, struggled to understand the concepts presented by her ninth grade science teacher. Hurt by her subpar academic performance in that class, she stated to her mother with exasperation, "Sometimes I feel like I'm the only one in the class who doesn't understand what the teacher is saying. It's embarrassing to feel so dumb."

Lucie's mother recognized that her daughter was being unnecessarily hard on herself. Lucie was not "dumb." Yet she also realized that at the moment Lucie was feeling inadequate. She knew that the time was not right to try to convince Lucie that she was smart, so she responded, "That science class is getting the best of you. That's an experience you haven't had very often in the past."

Seeing that Mother understood her, Lucie continued, "Sometimes I think I understand things, but when the teacher calls on me to answer, I can't think of what to say!"

"Kind of like your mind freezes? That's exasperating." Lucie nodded at her mother's correct interpretation.

"We have another test in 10 days. I really want to do well to try to get my average up." Lucie focused on how she could improve on her relatively poor standing in the class.

Seeing that her daughter had good intentions and did not need to be prodded in order to motivate herself, Lucie's mother felt a sense of comfort in her daughter's ability to overcome her problem. "Lucie, I'm glad to see you approaching this problem with a positive attitude. I'm anxious to see how you do on your next test."

Lucie benefited in a number of ways from this brief talk with her mother. Having been allowed by her mother to search for a solution to her own problem, Lucie expressed herself in a complete and honest fashion. Respect for Lucie's ability to make appropriate personal decisions was conveyed. Her emotional feelings of frustration and defeat were accepted as valid. As a result, Lucie's sensitivity to potential failure became a motivating factor for her rather than a stumbling block leading to self–doubt and personal questioning.

Provide compliments in a productive manner. In talking with parents of a sensitive child, I frequently hear the parents vow to make more of an effort to compliment or praise to their child. This internal promise comes in recognition of the child's need to develop a healthy sense of self–worth. I learned a valuable lesson about the way a child perceives parental praise from a young boy who was particularly sensitive and prone to self–doubt. One day in my office he told me, "My parents are constantly thinking of ways to tell me how great I am. They tell me I'm sweet or I'm smart, but I know I'm not. You can look at how much trouble I cause for everyone and see that I'm not nearly as good as they say I am."

After hearing this boy's statement, it was evident that he, like so many other children, was well aware of the accuracy of the compliments aimed at him. When his mother referred to him as "sweet," he rejected her praise knowing that sweet boys did not entertain the thoughts of guilt, anger, and shame that were inside him. He did not accept his father's description of him as "smart" because a smart boy would know how to make friends easier than he did. This child wanted to accept only those statements that he could readily verify as being accurate.

Because of this tendency to be overly interpretive of the words directed toward him, it is often important to be concrete in providing verbal reinforcement. The child should be given a statement that can be accepted at face value as being accurate.

- A child who has just helped clean the kitchen after a meal may be told, "The kitchen looks much nicer now that we've cleaned it up. Your help means a lot to me." Such a statement can be accepted even by a child who only infrequently seems to deserve a compliment. The child, then, can assume for himself that he is competent. The responsibility of drawing a conclusion about the child's worth as a person rests where it should—with the child.

Parent's Statement	Child's Inference
"Your help means a lot to me."	*I can make a contribution.*

Figure 8

- A teenager who has gone out of her way to help a fellow student who was struggling in an English class may be told, "You've put in a lot of time to help your friend understand her English assignments. To do that requires a lot of patience on your part." It is the teenager who must then take that true statement and use it to build positive self–worth. A sensitive teenager might have rejected a statement such as, "You are truly a good friend. People can always count on you." That pronouncement carries with it a judgment that may be unacceptable to one with a weak self–image.

Parent's Statement	Child's Inference
"You've spent a lot of time helping your friend."	*I can be a valuable companion.*

Figure 9

- A sensitive child is likely to accept a parent's comment that says, "Thanks for calling to let me know you are at Gladys' house. I feel more comfortable knowing where you are." Such a comment allows the child to assume for himself that he is capable of being responsible.

Parent's Statement	Child's Inference
"Thank you for calling to tell where you are. That makes me feel comfortable."	*I can be dependable.*

Figure 10

Matthew 16:13–20 is one of my favorite exchanges between Christ and His disciple, Peter. After Peter displayed his understanding that Jesus is the Messiah, Jesus complimented the disciple by predicting the good that would result from Peter's newfound knowledge. We can only imagine the affirmation Peter must have felt as his Teacher acknowledged Peter's value as a person. In a like manner, parents can seize opportunities to encourage their children and their developing personalities.

Help the child live within his own limits. Throughout our society, children and adolescents are continually encouraged to live an uninhibited, "wide open" life–style. I've heard many sensitive children bemoan the fact that they are shy and unassertive. They have unfortunately been duped into believing that to be themselves is not desirable. As these children reach their teenage years, they are faced with intense pressure to conform to the standards of the more vocal and noticeable members of their peer group.

Parents are in a prime position to acknowledge the importance of individuality. The parent who recognizes the value of individual differences can assist his child as he searches for self–acceptance. The parent who attempts to change the sensitive child becomes a stumbling block, discouraging the development of the child's personal growth.

—Case Study—

Ten–year–old David was brought to my office by his parents because of their growing concern for his apparent negative self–image. They explained (and David later confirmed) that their son felt unimportant in comparison to others. He did not feel his ideas were valued by his friends. In many ways he felt left out of the mainstream of activities enjoyed by his friends. His unhappiness had resulted in poor sleeping habits, regular bed–wetting, and frequent complaints of minor ailments such as headaches and stomachaches.

Later I learned that though he loved his son, Dad was greatly disappointed in David's lack of competitiveness and desire to win. As the third child with two older sisters, David provided the opportunity for Dad to enjoy his son's performance in competitive activities.

Dad had enrolled David in organized sports activities at the age of six. Thinking that his son needed to be driven hard to develop the aggressiveness necessary to become a winner, Dad spent many evening and weekend hours coaching an unwilling son on the finer aspects of athletics. Frustration was usually the result of these training sessions. David explained to me that many of his feelings of inadequacy came as a result of his chronic inability to satisfy his father's expectations.

To try to force a change in a child's personality will virtually always end in the creation of a problem. The child often concludes that there is something wrong with the way he is emotionally constructed. The ironic result is that the child is then more likely to experience an exaggeration of the qualities that others have convinced him are negative.

A parent helps the sensitive child to live within his personality limits by following these guidelines:

- Refrain from using labels that may be construed negatively, such as "shy" or "quiet."

- Provide opportunities that allow the child to be noticed without placing pressure on him, such as having him serve guests or quietly pointing out his accomplishments to others.

- Use reinforcements and rewards abundantly. Make sparse use of criticism.

- Listen when the child is discouraged.

- Create opportunities where the child can experience success. Learn the things that the child is good at.

- Demonstrate patience with others who may be perceived as "different."

Summary

Sensitivity can be a domineering personality characteristic that can result in difficult behavior patterns. Because of a highly sensitive nature, emotions may be experienced in an intense manner. The primary traits displayed by the sensitive child include:

- A tendency to be overly self–conscious of how others react to him.

- The withholding of emotions in an inappropriate way causing a lack of proper assertiveness.

- Resistance from emotional independence with a tendency to become too dependent on others.

- A fragile self–esteem that lends the child toward developing a poor self–image.

- Hiding emotions by acting socially inappropriate.

Various factors may have an influence on the way in which a child's sensitive nature is displayed. The interaction of these variables will determine their ultimate expression.

- Inborn personality characteristics may make a child more sensitive than others.

- Though sensitivity is not a negative characteristic, the responses a sensitive child receives from others can encourage the development of potentially negative behavior patterns.

- Some sensitive children succumb to the pressure of expectations that are too strong for them to successfully meet.

- The lack of opportunity for the sensitive child to communicate effectively with others can create barriers to emotional growth.

Managing the sensitive child begins with a thorough understanding of the factors shaping the child's emotional and behavioral expression. With a healthy grasp of the child's personality, guidance can be given to help shape it in a positive direction.

- Though it is often tempting to shield a sensitive child from emotional discomfort, it is important to use judgment in allowing the child to learn natural control over his own disposition.

- Avoid the inviting lure to become responsible for the choices a sensitive child should make. To depend too strongly on others can become a liability for the child.

- Communication with the child begins with good listening techniques, allowing the child to draw conclusions about his own strengths and weaknesses.

- Well–timed and properly stated verbal reinforcement can serve to build a strong self–image within the child.

- Parents can help the sensitive child come to self–acceptance by helping him live within his own limitations.

Session 1

Study Session Objective:

To identify patterns of sensitivity in your child and learn how these patterns could contribute to emotional harm.

Biblical Reference: 1 Tim. 4:11–16

Paul offers guidance to young Timothy. The tenderness with which Paul treats his relationship with Timothy may communicate as much about Timothy's disposition as Paul's loving counsel. Note how Paul encourages him to use his personal strengths to their fullest extent.

Discussion Questions:

1. What positive qualities does your sensitive child possess? Have some of these qualities become out of balance? In what ways?

2. How observant of others is your child? Does he have a tendency to take things the wrong way?

3. What do you do to ease the emotional discomfort your child may experience? By doing so, has your child become more dependent on you? What reactions do you give the child that may inadvertently encourage him to be less responsible for his own feelings?

4. What does your child's behavior communicate about how he feels about himself? Are there emotions your child experiences but cannot talk about? In what ways are these emotions expressed?

5. How does your child use his emotional softness as a manipulative tool? What could be the long–term effects of this emotional pattern?

Assignments:

1. Observe the ways in which your child's sensitivity allows him to be excused from some responsibilities. Make a list of your observations. If you feel bold, make a second list of the con-

cessions you give to your child so he won't experience further emotional discomfort.

2. Incorporate the phrases, "That's something you can do," and "You are capable of doing that by yourself," into your communication with your sensitive child. Watch how your child resists your efforts to encourage independence. Write down what you learn from these interactions about how your child draws you into behavior patterns that could damage the child's self–confidence.

Session 2

Study Session Objective:

To begin to create positive qualities of sensitivity from negative ones through the use of effective communication and discipline.

Biblical Reference: Rom. 15:1–13

Paul encourages his readers to be imitators of Christ. Apply these teachings to your family relationships. Use these words to build your resolve to strengthen the needs of your child.

Discussion Questions:

1. What are your greatest fears of what might eventually become of your sensitive child? In what ways do you communicate these fears to your child?

2. When you try to communicate assurance to your child, how does he react? Does he fully understand you when you point out his good qualities? Does he reject your efforts to boost his self–concept? How does your child interpret your actions toward him?

3. How badly do you hurt when your child experiences emotional discomfort? How "high" do you get when he has positive experiences? To what degree does your child take advantage of your emotional investment in him?

4. How closely attuned are you to the messages your child sends through his behavioral expression? How well do you communicate to your child your understanding of these emotions?

Assignments:

1. Take a few minutes during the next few days to casually observe your child as he interacts with others. Note how his self–concept is reflected in his behavior. Use this experience as a learning tool that teaches you the self–concept needs of your child.

2. Select one chore you routinely do for your child that he is capable of doing (e.g., taking his dirty dishes to the kitchen sink or making his bed). Have him do this chore. Continually work on developing independence within the child.

3

What, *Me* Worry?—

The Anxious Child

Most ADULTS would have considered nine–year–old Angie an easy–to–manage child. She was a quiet girl, so quiet that she was often considered shy. At school she was always compliant. She followed all the rules and was very seldom corrected for misbehavior. Even though she was a quiet child, the other children seemed to like her.

Despite her generally pleasant nature, Angie's parents described their daughter as a perplexing child. As she did at school, she followed the rules at home without difficulty. In many ways, she was a perfectionist about keeping her room straightened and about her personal appearance.

Yet, Angie's fearfulness bothered her parents. On many mornings Angie whined and complained about having to go to school. She could not give an explanation for her reluctance other than to say she did not like school. She had similar difficulties when her parents left her with a babysitter, or when she spent the night at the house of a friend. Anything that deviated from the normal routine upset Angie.

Complaints of stomachaches were common with Angie. Even though her parents often felt the girl was just feigning illness for attention, they made regular trips to the doctor's office for reassurance. His recommendation was always the same—Angie simply needed to confront her fears.

Disagreement between Mom and Dad became more common. Dad advocated a hard–line approach to solving the girl's problem. Mom felt sorry for Angie and tried to find ways to soothe her worries. Neither approach worked as Angie continued in a pattern of meekness. Beneath the facade of composure that Angie publicly portrayed, her parents knew their daughter harbored unexplained anxieties.

Defining the Anxious Child

Anxiety is one of those terms we often hear but do not fully understand. Anxiety absorbs many different emotions to form a complex range of behaviors. Most often we think of anxiety as involving worry. Indeed, worry plays a major role in anxiety development, but so do factors such as stress, fear, self–esteem, and the child's natural temperament.

Christ told His followers that worry is unnecessary because man's needs will most certainly be provided for by their loving Heavenly Father (Matt. 6:26–34). Children, however, lack the capacity to fully comprehend this promise. Childhood anxiety that goes unchecked can lead that young person into a life–style that is without the assurance of God's protection over His prize creation. Parental understanding of this child's emotional struggle is the first step in guiding him to greater personal contentment and comfort.

Parents who have an anxious child feel particularly baffled by that child's behavior. Many parents of such children express frustration that other adults fail to recognize the complexity of their child's ways. A teacher told the parent of one anxious child, "Oh, don't worry about your son. He is going to be fine. Sure, he's a little shy and he doesn't speak up a whole lot, but he will outgrow it. They always do."

That parent explained to me, "I know my son's teacher meant well, but I don't think she realizes how intense his behavior can be. He doesn't think he can do anything right. He's scared to death he is going to make a mistake and be laughed at by the other children. I wish she could see him at home and hear the things he tells me. Then she might not be so sure that this is just a phase he is going through."

Anxiety appears to be equally common in both boys and girls. Some experts argue, however, that because of the way our society encourages girls to accept passive, dependent roles, this condition is more frequent in females. For some children and adolescents, anxiety seems to be a permanent part of their life—style. For others, anxious states may be only temporary and result from a reaction to specific circumstances. An examination of the most common elements of this condition follows.

The child reacts to stress in a personal way. Stress is a difficult term to quantify. We have all experienced stress in varying degrees during our lifetimes. Yet, what is stressful to one person may be stimulating to another. Personal temperament style, past experience, and other factors determine how stressful an event or circumstance may be. Thus, it is not always an easy matter to predict when a child or adolescent may react with anxiety to a potentially stressful situation.

My own dealings with young people have led me to conclude that in the early years of life, children derive their greatest source of emotional comfort (or emotional distress) from their families. The way family members, especially parents, respond to stress may have a strong bearing on the eventual anxiety level of the child. As the child reaches the teenage years, other social factors play a prominent role in the level of emotional comfort the young person experiences. Even at that age, however, the relationships at home play an important part in the teenager's internal stress level. The anxious child will respond with intensity to family stress.

—Case Study—

At age 10, Mark had developed a long history of anxiety that went beyond normal boundaries. He was difficult to manage and often seemed to be hyperactive. His unpredictable moods often resulted in emotional explosions that occurred with little advanced notice.

Several interviews with Mark revealed how closely his emotions were tied to the status of his parents' marriage. He was more keenly aware of the tension that existed between his parents than they realized.

In the privacy of my office, Mark described with accurate detail the mood of each parent when they were at odds with one another. Although Mom and Dad tried to avoid airing their differences before their children, Mark could always tell when they were upset with one another. He noticed the lack of direct eye contact between his parents. The sharp responses given by one parent to the other were a signal that something was wrong. He explained that his dad worked in the yard or performed other odd jobs to let off some of his frustration.

In response to the tension between his parents, Mark reacted by becoming more emotional. Although his poor behavior often met criticism or punishment, his intention was to draw attention to the discomfort he felt inside. He refrained from verbalizing this source of his stress, but his behavior showed just how keenly aware he was of the status of his parents' relationship. In a telling statement, he said to me, "When my mom and dad are upset, I feel like screaming, but I can't because I don't know what to say. Besides, I am not supposed to scream so I just hold it inside. It hurts!"

A strained marital relationship caused Mark's parents to be more irritable, less communicative, and less affectionate with one another. In turn, Mark felt the ill effects of their relationship in the form of a more negative home environment. The discomfort of seeing his parents at odds with one another encouraged an anxious response in the boy. Feeling incapable of telling his parents the emotions he felt, Mark reacted negatively. He felt tense and could not relax. While he appeared to be a hyperactive child, it was actually his internal unrest that caused his behavior problems. The conflict between his parents resulted in internal conflict for Mark that manifested itself in the form of anxiety.

Many apparently nonthreatening situations may be overemphasized. While virtually all children show some anxiety in response to stressful circumstances, some children have an exaggerated reaction to relatively normal situations. In many cases fear is the result of self–doubt. A child or teenager's lack of self–confidence can push him to transfer his fears onto a harmless circumstance. It is common for the anxious child to suffer from low self–esteem. A child who doubts himself is prone to assume the worst. He also assumes that since he rates himself in a negative manner, others will, too.

Ironically, the anxious child may be his own worst enemy. Because he is fearful and lacking in confidence, he is tentative as he approaches life's daily demands. Others recognize this self–doubt and fail to give him the affirmation he needs in order to build upon his confidence. A negative cycle develops that entraps the increasingly helpless victim of anxiety.

Following are examples of how an anxious child may over-react to situations that are relatively normal:

- A 13–year–old girl reluctantly attends a party given by one of her friends. There are several other teenagers present whom she has not previously met. Because she is convinced that she will not be well received by the newcomers, she participates minimally in the party's activities. She explains to a concerned friend that she does not feel well.

- Upon returning home from school each day, an elementary school child demands much attention from his mother and seems to be unable to complete simple chores or homework assignments without constant supervision. His real fear, however, is that his younger sister may get more attention than he receives. He does not want to lose his place within the family.

- A 15–year–old boy loses his temper regularly over matters that seem to be petty. On the same day, he blew up at his sister for listening to a radio station he disliked, his mother for not having supper prepared on time, and at the family dog for jumping up on him as he walked into the backyard.

- Informed that her playmate could not play, a five–year–old child cries and complains, "Nancy doesn't like me. She doesn't want to play with me." No amount of reasoning by her mother can console the girl.

- The move to a new school has a frightful effect on a sixth–grade boy. Upset by the change in his life, it takes the child much longer to adjust than would normally be expected. The adjustment period is so difficult for him that his grades decline sharply.

In each of these examples, a situation that most children would manage with minimal difficulty became a trauma for the anxious child. That child's interpretation of the event caused him to look at the potential for harm and to ignore simple solutions to the given dilemma. The anxious child may develop habits that follow him throughout childhood and adolescence. In many ways the child anticipates a negative result and thus serves to encourage that result to come about. In a spiraling fashion he overreacts to daily circumstances causing his own fearfulness to grow. The anxious child becomes, then, his own worst enemy.

—Case Study—

Vince was a 15–year–old boy about whom his parents had grown increasingly concerned. Although a sensitive child, his demands upon his family had grown unbearable during his teen years. When he was younger, his parents could usually satisfy his desires and avoid the emotional outbursts that had now become more common. Vince had come to feel that he was a burden to his family and had an uneasy feeling that his place in the family was not secure. As a young boy he was able to be pacified by extra treats, privileges, or attention. However, rather than reduce the demands on his parents as a result of their responsiveness to him, Vince raised his expectations for them as he grew older.

Mr. and Mrs. Hull, Vince's parents, provided a long list of examples of the irrational expectations their son had for them. Despite his young age, Vince wanted to drive the family car. He was not content to drive on isolated roads with his father's supervision, but expected the car to be given to him on Friday nights as well. When it was suggested that Vince earn money for his own entertainment by offering to do yard work for his neighbors, Vince refused to talk to his neighbors unless his dad accompanied him. And when he found work to do, he insisted that his father help because of his own fear of failure. His mother had given up all hope that Vince would learn to take care of his own basic needs. The complaints from him were overbearing whenever she asked for help doing his laundry, cleaning up after himself, and performing other simple chores. In Vince's way of thinking, a caring parent would not make him do so much work.

At the root of Vince's increasingly difficult behavior pattern was a fear of how others evaluated him. He felt unimportant if he was not shown a lot of attention. He felt personally rejected when his requests were not fulfilled. He failed to notice the impractical nature of his demands on others and continued a relentless pursuit aimed at making himself feel more secure in his relationships with others.

Mr. and Mrs. Hull had no intention of encouraging the development of anxiety in their son. By frequently giving in to Vince's demands, their hope was that he would be satisfied and would not feel the need to continue asking for special treatment. Yet, Vince's own preoccupation with his place of importance in his family and peer group caused the continuation of his behavior and resulted in increased feelings of anxiety and worry.

A variety of demanding behaviors may be displayed by an anxious child as he seeks reassurance from others. Some of the more common expressions of this characteristic are as follows:

- Consistently misinterprets what others say and do.

- Overly sensitive to remarks meant as constructive criticism.

- Displays emotional outbursts that are stronger than the situation calls for.

- Won't let go of comments that were made in passing or were not intended to be taken seriously.

- Expresses doubt that others will live up to their word.

- Makes frequent statements suggesting self–doubt and low self–confidence.

- Becomes preoccupied with concerns that others consider to be minor.

- Asks the same questions over and over.
- Wants proof that others mean what they say.
- Feels rejected when attention is shown to others.

While many would interpret the demands of an anxious child as mere arrogance, this behavior suggests self–doubt rather than the excessive self–assurance that accompanies arrogance. To be sure, an anxious child may become self–centered as a result of having his demands consistently met. Yet, there never develops the quality of true brashness and egotism that so often is seen in the narcissistic child or teenager. The anxious child is concerned about how others evaluate him.

The desire to comply results in indecisiveness. While many children and adolescents who experience anxiety may be demanding, others are compliant and easy to get along with. Rather than seek reassurance of their worth by making demands based on unrealistic expectations, some anxious children attempt to soothe their self–doubt by doing precisely what is expected of them. A word of approval provides a momentary sense of relief from the frequent fear of not pleasing others.

In the eyes of many parents, the anxious behavior of their child is most perplexing. In so many ways, the young person appears to be in agreement with his world, but the unhappiness that periodically engulfs him is difficult to explain.

A source of discomfort for the anxious child results from having to be decisive. Wanting badly to please others, the child feels great internal tension when called upon to make a decision he knows will not please everyone. Examples of the degree to which this form of anxiety can pose problems to children are illustrated as follows:

- While studying a unit on past presidents of the United States, 11–year–old Todd has difficulty deciding which president he will make the focus of an assigned report.

    Todd's mother thinks he should study a contemporary president since it will help him develop an understanding of modern day politics. Todd, however, is more interested in

Thomas Jefferson. Not wanting to offend his mother, Todd procrastinates and fails to begin his project until two days before it is due. Although he follows his own inclination and reports on Thomas Jefferson's presidency, he makes a poor grade due to a hastily prepared assignment. In the end, he feels guilty that he did not follow his mother's suggestion.

Anxious Behavior	Emotional Fear	Result
• Procrastination in completing an assignment.	• Afraid of offending Mother.	• Guilt over poor grades.

Figure 11

• Denise spends alternate weekends with her father who is divorced from Denise's mother. One weekend she has been invited to spend the night with a friend. She wants to be with her friend, but she fears that her father will be disappointed with her if she asks him to change their scheduled visit. Her friend assumes that Denise will spend the night with her. On Friday morning before the given weekend, Denise reluctantly calls her dad. Dad is agreeable to the change but chides Denise for waiting until the last minute to inform him of her plans. That night Denise talks negatively about herself to her friend and fails to have the fun she originally anticipated.

Anxious Behavior	Emotional Fear	Result
• Refrains from informing Dad.	• Father might be disappointed.	• Feels irresponsible.

Figure 12

• On a Saturday afternoon, Janie and her best friend decide to go to a movie. Janie has no money and is certain her parents do not have the extra cash. She does not want to admit to her friend that she does not have the money to go to the movies because she is afraid of what her friend might think of her family. Rather than tell her friend of her dilemma, Janie acts indecisive about which movie she would like to see. Finally, as friend must cancel their plans because they waited too long to make a decision.

Anxious Behavior	Emotional Fear	Result
• Delays in making a decision.	• Friend might think less of her.	• Evasive communication.

Figure 13

In each of the previous illustrations (see figures 11–13) the anxious child presented a behavior pattern that was difficult for others to deal with. The irony of the behavior lies in the fact that it was problematic because the child wanted too much to please others. The concern these children have for others creates a tension within that often renders that child helpless.

The indecisive quality of many anxious children yields several negative results for the child. Some of the more common results are listed here:

- The value of responsibility is diminished in the eyes of the child.

- Others look upon the child as unreliable.

- Creative alternatives to problem solving are ignored.

- A sense of accomplishment is seldom experienced by the child.

- Skills are not developed to their fullest potential.

- The young person learns to be fearful of anything new.

- By wanting so badly to please everyone, the child pleases no one.

- Communication with others becomes vague.

- The child suffers a lack of self–esteem because little confidence is shown in him by others.

- The child disregards his own feelings.

- Others learn to take advantage of the child's good nature.

The quality of indecisiveness found in many anxious children and adolescents is an example of a characteristic that becomes a liability because it is unbalanced. Armed with the unrealistic hope of being all things to all people, the child faces a no–win situation that results in constant tension. Rather than use the sensitivity that causes him to want to get along well with others to his advantage, the young person becomes mired in a stagnant life–style that results in unhappiness.

Separation from significant persons may be difficult. Because fear is at the root of the emotion of anxiety, the potential loss of a secure, close relationship can be a frightening prospect to the anxious child. The relationship between such a young person and his parents often becomes the most important relationship the child has. While it is natural for the child to feel a sense of dependence upon his mother and father for emotional security, the anxious child may become overly dependent. The child may misinterpret the parents' encouragement of independent activity as a withdrawal of their emotional support.

It is common for young children to experience short–term anxiety when separated from a parent. Yet an intensely fearful response to separation from a significant figure signals an anxiety that goes beyond normal boundaries. This separation anxiety may not be seen until a child reaches the preadolescent years indicating that this emotion is capable of building over a period of years until it reaches unmanageable proportions.

—Case Study—

By the time 12–year–old Adam had reached the seventh grade he had achieved a high degree of success. He was a member of the student council at his junior high school and enjoyed a good reputation among his teachers. He was a strong student who frequently was named on the school's honor role. He had enrolled in the school band and showed promise as a trumpet player. He had a number of friends with whom he associated after school and on weekends.

Adam attended what was known in the community as a rough school. A predominance of students came from economically deprived homes. Though fights were common among the students, Adam had never been involved in an argument with another student. In fact, Adam's mother had been told by the principal that her son was one of the school heroes because of his well–rounded personality and school behavior.

During the first weeks of each school year, Adam complained daily to his mother that he did not want to go to school. The complaints varied but contained the same element of fear. He complained that he was unprepared for a test, or that he would not be able to complete the assignments given during the day. Despite these fears, Adam always managed to do well academically.

Similarly, Adam often expressed concern for his relationships with other students. He was certain that others disliked him because he was not particularly athletic. He worried that somehow he might become a victim of the frequent conflicts among other students. Again, none of his fears proved to be valid.

The seventh–grade year was different for Adam. While in the past he experienced a variety of concerns at the beginning of each school year, he had always overcome them several weeks into the year. But in this particular year, not only did Adam's fears fail to subside with time, they intensified.

By the end of the first half of the year, Adam had missed 16 days from school. He had become a social recluse due to his increasing discomfort among his peer group. He insisted that his mother stay near him when they were away from home and had thrown numerous temper tantrums when his mother had insisted that he attend school. Adam's dependence on her had reached an unhealthy level and caused her to become quite concerned for her son.

There are times that anxiety within a child may reach a sense of terror. As in Adam's case, worries may run away from the child as he becomes preoccupied with circumstances or events that are beyond his control. In an effort to gain control over his own anxiety, the child may desperately cling to a parent.

In cases of separation anxiety, the anticipation of the dreaded event is almost always worse than the actual event itself. Expecting a frightful experience, the child may resort to a wide range of behaviors that are not normally seen in him. In Adam's case, this normally subdued, well–mannered child threw unusually strong tantrums, shouting words and phrases that were out of character for him. His need to remain both physically and emotionally close to his mother underscored the intensity of the fearful nature within him.

Symptoms of physical discomfort may appear. I am convinced that there is a close connection between how individuals feel about themselves emotionally and how they feel physically. This belief in the link between mind and body not only applies to adults, but to children and adolescents as well. Each child has an optimum level of emotional discomfort that can be tolerated without harmful physical side effects. Yet once the stress level passes that point of tolerance, the body reacts in a negative way. Thus, a traumatic event or a series of events can cause physical discomfort within the child's body.

One characteristic of humans that separates us from lower forms of life is our ability to think and feel in a complex manner. This ability can cause a child to carry the burden of anxiety within himself years after a traumatic event has occurred. For example, I remember counseling a 14–year–old boy who routinely became queasy when he attended baseball games because of being hit in the back by a foul ball when attending a game as a young child. His ability to recall the fear associated with that event caused its effect to last much longer than might otherwise have been predicted.

The development of physical symptoms that appear to have no medical basis is often a sign of anxiety that is out of control. Note the more common complaints made by anxious children and adolescents:

- Nervous stomach accompanied by gas, nausea, or diarrhea.
- Chronic tension headaches or even migraine headaches.
- Feelings of fatigue despite adequate rest and nourishment.
- Wetting or soiling of clothing.
- Sleep disturbances such as insomnia, fitful rest, nightmares, or night terrors.
- Low tolerance to minor scrapes or injuries.
- Low–grade fever associated with stomachaches or headaches.
- Shortness of breath or hyperventilation.
- Feelings of dizziness or faintness.
- Increased blood pressure or heart rate.

While not all occurrences of these physical symptoms are directly related to anxiety, it is certainly wise to recognize the way in which a child's body may give important clues about his emotional well being. A negative change in a child's mood and behavior accompanied by physical symptoms of discomfort is a strong hint that the child is feeling tense and anxious.

Factors Influencing the Anxious Child's Behavior

Too much pressure may produce an anxious response. The pressure a child feels from his world may take a variety of forms. There is pressure to succeed in school, to fit in with a peer group, to meet the demands of authority figures, and live up to the expectations of others. A certain degree of pressure can be healthy for a child, for it provides a challenge that motivates the young person to be productive. Life with no demands leads to inefficiency and chronic boredom. Of course, a healthy balance must be maintained between no stimulation at all and pressure that is overwhelming. As parents, we often place pressure on our children hoping it will provide positive motivation. Yet, an overzealous parent may create enough stress on a child so as to create a burden of anxiety that becomes debilitating.

—Case Study—

Ten–year–old Julia had taken piano lessons since she was a second grader. Now in her fourth year of study, Julia had developed some proficiency on this instrument. Her mother was also an accomplished pianist and took pride in the progress of her daughter. It was Mother's hope that through the development of her musical abilities, Julia could earn a scholarship to college and go on to a rewarding career in the field of music. In light of this desire, Mother thought it was in Julia's best interest to push her to the limit in order to maximize her budding potential.

A rigorous schedule of piano rehearsal was developed for Julia. Before school each morning the child focused on technique and music theory. After school she worked on expanding her musical repertoire and polishing her style. As Julia grew older, the practice times were lengthened. By the time Julia was 14 years old, she played the piano two to three hours per day. Even with these extended practices, there seemed to be so much that she needed to learn. Wanting to please her demanding, but well–meaning mother, Julia persisted in her playing, but lost her enthusiasm for the instrument.

In a departure from her earlier years, the teenaged Julia became more resistant toward her mother. The two frequently argued about her piano technique. Julia could no longer muster the effort needed to complete her demanding practice schedule. When her mother tutored her, Julia often felt such internal pressure to meet her mother's expectations that she could not play the piano suitably. Her emotions became fragile. This once strong girl now crumbled quickly when given constructive criticism. She openly stated that she hated the piano. She complained of being so tense that she could not sleep at night. Her concentration on other important activities, mainly school responsibilities, suffered greatly. In short, Julia's life was characterized by excessive anxiety.

Anxiety is an emotion that may build over a number of years. In earlier years, a child may respond favorably to demands that are made. In Julia's case, she readily accepted the strain of a strict practice schedule as a young child. The constant, high expectations began to erode her self–esteem, but the degrading process did not have its full impact until several years later.

The parent is in a position to regulate the flow of pressure placed on a child. In fact, the parent is often responsible for placing the child under too much pressure. Well–intended goals, hopes, and expectations for a child can be transferred to a destructive pattern of pressure and demands upon that child. The end result of such a cycle is often anxiety.

Overprotectiveness can create anxiety. In the same way that an overbearing parent may create a feeling of anxiety within a child, an overly protective parent may foster this same emotion. Most individuals would define overprotectiveness as a circumstance in which the parent cautiously guards the child from as many of life's trials as possible. While guardedness is certainly present in many overprotective parents, another strong characteristic is also present—becoming too emotionally invested in the life of the child. Thus, the overly protective parent finds it difficult to separate his own emotions from those of the young person.

Overprotection of children may be shown in a variety of ways. Some illustrations of this behavior are as follows:

- Upon hearing that her child has made a poor grade on a test at school, a mother calls the teacher to complain about unfair testing procedures. The mother explains that the exam must have been too difficult since the child demonstrated a thorough knowledge of the subject matter the night before.

- Hating to see his daughter suffer the punishment he had administered earlier in the day, Dad tells the girl he will forget her misdeed this time, but cautions her to be careful the next time or he will not be so lenient.

- Following an argument with a neighbor, a boy seeks the comfort of his mother whom he knows will take his side on the issue. As he explains to his mother what happened, he dresses up the story to make it sound worse than it actually was. Mother accepts her son's explanation without verifying his story with others. She promises she will do all within her power to prevent such an incident from occurring again.

- Despite the fact that their teenage daughter has a job of her own, her parents continue to pay for all of her physical and social needs and provide her a car allowance. They rationalize that their child will only be a teenager once and that they want her to use her money in any way she pleases.

In each of these examples, parents have increased the likelihood of an anxious reaction within the child. Failure to allow the child to learn about his world through experience can produce a hesitancy within that young person to confront situations, needs, and people with a sense of confidence. The child can learn that when troubles arise, whether they are in the form of school demands, peer pressures, or financial constraints, someone will always step in to assure him of smooth sailing.

At some point in time, each child will face the need to confront the demands of life in an assertive manner. Those children and teenagers who have not been carefully taught the value of dealing with the daily concerns of life will more likely be struck with the fear that accompanies anxiety than those who have been allowed, within proper limits, to experience both the good and bad that life has to offer. The overinvestment of the parent that encourages him to shield the child from the consequences of life may surface in the form of a child without a sense of confidence or direction.

Children can learn anxiety through observing an anxious parent. There is both good news and bad news concerning how parents influence the development of behavioral habits within their children. The good news is that of all the people in the entire world, it is the parent who exerts the greatest influence on the way a child behaves, thinks, and feels.

The bad news in that since the child views the parent as a primary role model, the parent may inadvertently display behaviors, thoughts, or emotions that adversely influence the child.

I often find that anxiety in children is a learned behavior and is frequently demonstrated by one or both parents. It is uncanny how children from a very young age recognize and imitate the emotions of the adults in the family. The dependent nature of the child causes him to look to adults for cues on how to handle life's stressors.

—Case Study—

Gil and his mother, Mrs. Campbell, sat together in my office. Gil was a ten–year–old boy who calmly described to me a variety of his fears that painted a picture of childhood anxiety. He explained that it had become increasingly difficult for him to fall asleep at night. As he lay in bed, he tended to review the activities of his day and second–guessed many of the choices he had made. For example, he often wondered if he had completed a school assignment according to his teacher's desire, or questioned his judgment in the way he talked with a neighborhood friend earlier in the day.

Mrs. Campbell expressed her own uncertainty about how to deal with her son. She told Gil regularly that he worried too much. She felt he had become a perfectionist and expected too much of himself. None of the talking and reasoning Mrs. Campbell engaged in with the boy seemed to make a difference in him. Despite her efforts he continued to grow more anxious daily. She was worried that his lack of confidence would build to a harmful crescendo.

As we explored the dynamic structure of this family, it became apparent that Mrs. Campbell had many of the anxious qualities that were emerging in her son. She described herself as a perfectionist in her own right. She believed that to do less than her best on a task might expose her to the criticism of others. A socially aware individual, Mrs. Campbell wanted to be liked by virtually all people with whom she had contact. She thought it was important to teach Gil the virtues of dependability and responsibility and regularly talked to him about these matters.

Mrs. Campbell had a healthy idea of behavior patterns she wished to establish in her son. Yet, through both word and deed, she had carried this positive concept a step too far so that Gil became overly anxious. Exchanges between mother and child caused Gil to doubt that he was living up to parental expectations. His personal sense of competence had grown less certain as he grew older. Additionally, his mother's routine display of her own doubt and uncertainty encouraged Gil to wonder if there would ever come a point in his maturity that he could quit chasing the elusive dream of perfection.

Children, especially at a young age, want to be like their mothers or fathers. It is natural for them to imitate the behaviors, thoughts, and beliefs displayed by their parents. Because modeling of parental behavior plays such an important part in the child's behavioral development, it is essential to examine this factor as answers are sought for the child's emotional and behavioral tendencies.

Children may be predisposed to anxiety. In discussing other behavior patterns of childhood and adolescence, it has been explained that an infant enters the world with his own personality agenda. I like to view each child as having a blueprint for personality that may be built upon by the experiences life offers. While the boundaries of each child's life determine many of the characteristics that make that child unique, his own temperament in many ways dictates how he will interpret the events of his childhood.

My experience with children and adolescents has led me to conclude that anxiety–prone children often possess characteristics similar to children who have a sensitive nature. These often compliant, likable, and sociable young people are in their own way as difficult to raise as a more blatantly oppositional child. The easy going child may lull the parent into a pattern of response that initially seems harmless but eventually results in emotional immaturity and fearfulness. I have often told a guilt–ridden parent that it is not necessarily his parental style which is wrong. A child may develop an anxious condition as a result of a mismatch between the parents' behaviors and the child's personality, neither of which is bad when viewed separately.

Parental response styles that fail to match the personality needs of anxiety–prone children may include:

- Tentatively voicing demands to the child because he seems too fragile to treat firmly.

- Showering the child with affection because he is so responsive.

- Making exceptions to rules because the child seems to have already experienced sufficient remorse.

- Doing things for the child that he is capable of doing on his own.

- Failing to give recognition to a child who seems to be so self–reliant.

- Overlooking behavior that could intensify if left unchecked.

- Feeling sorry for the child when he cries or becomes upset.

- Giving the child "adult" responsibilities at too young an age.

Of course, the parent who responds to his child in any of these ways does not intend to provoke anxiety. It must be remembered, however, that the anxious child is one who tends to keep his feelings to himself. He does not want to be a nuisance to anyone for fear of rejection by those upon whom he is so dependent.

As parents we have a tendency to assume that either all is well with our child if problems are not outwardly apparent, or that the verbal and emotional expressions of our child represent an honest view of all thoughts and feelings he holds within. Frequently those well–intentioned assumptions may entice us into response patterns that seem to be effective in the short run. Over a long period of time, however, responses that include inconsistency, overindulgence, pity, or indecisiveness may work against our best intentions to provide for our child's emotional needs.

A sensitive child has that special emotional appeal that can sweep his parents into a whirlwind of emotions causing decisions to be made based on the child's immediate wishes rather than his long-term needs. Well-meaning parental generosity can contribute to emotional uncertainty in the child. The result may be unexpected anxiety.

The reaction of others may produce a powerful feeling. The word *power* is often a key term in explaining the behavior of a child. To the oppositional child, power usually translates into control, a feeling that is most gratifying. In contrast to the oppositional child, the anxious child has little desire to be in control of others. He is satisfied to follow the lead of more assertive individuals. He normally does not enjoy activities or relationships that involve risk.

Yet, despite this general dislike for power struggles, the anxious child may learn through experience that certain behaviors can offer a sense of control over the fearful circumstances of life. The anxious child who engages adults in power struggles may do so only after he learns that in so doing he can avoid what he fears. This momentary power over fear can become an addictive feeling which produces a negative cycle of anxiety.

—Case Study—

Bonnie's friend, Melissa, called to invite her to spend Friday night at her house. Melissa excitedly gave Bonnie the details of her plans for their time together. First, the girls would have pizza with Melissa's parents. After dinner, they would play several games, listen to music, and read magazines. Bonnie quickly became as excited as Melissa and told her she could not wait for Friday night to arrive.

On Friday afternoon Bonnie began to feel apprehensive about her plans to stay overnight with Melissa. She approached her mother with her concern. "Mom, I'm not real sure I want to spend the night at Melissa's house tonight. I may just stay home instead."

"What? You've looked forward to this night all week. You can't back out now! That wouldn't be fair to Melissa."

"But Mom, you know I hate to sleep at someone else's house. Melissa's house is too close to the bus station. There are too many strange people roaming around their neighborhood. I don't feel safe at night in their house."

Mom was becoming perturbed at her daughter. "Oh, Bonnie, you've never said you were afraid of Melissa's neighborhood before. That's just an excuse. Now quit talking like that and go get your things ready. You know you'll have a good time tonight."

Bonnie refused to let go of her fear. "Mom you're not listening to me. I do not want to go! Just call Melissa's mother and tell her I'm sick. I'm not going!"

The struggle between Bonnie and her mom progressed throughout the afternoon. Bonnie repeatedly expressed her fear of spending the night away from home while Mom persistently attempted to persuade Bonnie that her fears were unfounded. Eventually Bonnie agreed to spend the night at her friend's house, but only after she had gained some concessions from her Mom. Mom agreed to linger at Melissa's house for a while so Bonnie could feel assured that she was safe. It was also agreed that Mom would go straight home from Melissa's house so that Bonnie could reach her by phone if necessary. Bonnie further received a promise from her mother to call Melissa's house before bedtime to give Bonnie a word of comfort. Though it was a struggle for both mother and daughter, Bonnie made it through the night without harm, though she shared that she had been a nervous wreck.

During the struggle, Bonnie had no intention of exerting power over her mom. To be sure, she used emotional power tactics and manipulation, but her goal was to control *her fears* rather than to control her mom. Her plan was to draw her mom into her problem to such a degree that she could cause Mom to take Bonnie's problem as her own and help in solving it. By coercing her mom to provide concessions, Bonnie felt that she was no longer solely responsible for her anxiety. Mom had become a partner in Bonnie's dilemma.

While it was Mom's hope that her intervention would ease her daughter's fears, Bonnie's anxiety continued. Rather than learn to confront her fears assertively, Bonnie learned to shift her problems to others' shoulders if possible. In the end, the result was a continual spiral of untamed anxiety.

Childhood burnout can result in anxiety. Adults often tell me that they are tired of the life–styles they lead. Many of us have allowed ourselves to become overextended to such a degree that we are not sure if we are coming or going. The damage done to the harried adult is well–chronicled. The adult may experience depression, guilt, anxiety, and a host of stress–related physical ailments and conditions. This condition is commonly called "burnout."

In our fast–paced world, we are now recognizing the same effects of burnout in children as is seen in adults. At one point in time it was not considered likely or even possible that a child could become "burned out" on life. Perhaps one reason children are overlooked in this regard is that young people are in many ways more adaptable to changing events than are adults. Because childhood and adolescence is a time of rapid change and development in personality growth, young people may be more pliable in life situations which call for flexibility. Yet, a prolonged life–style of stressful circumstances can create the harmful side effect of childhood burnout.

Factors which contribute to the anxiety associated with burnout may include:

- *Overcommitment of a child's time to a variety of activities.* I know one burned out 12–year–old boy who is involved in the following activities: tennis lessons, school soccer team, church choir and hand bell ensembles, Boy Scouts, golf lessons, and frequent social activities with his friends. He also is an honor student at school. His life–style is so demanding that at his young age he has developed a peptic ulcer.

- *Outside pressure for the child to achieve.* Often children experience burnout due to their desire to meet the expectations placed on them. I once counseled a burned out teenager who was a moderately successful ice skater. As this teen grew older, she wanted to try other activities, but felt pressured by her family to continue in this single sport. Fear of disappointing family members led the girl to suppress her desires. Emotionally she became encumbered with resentment, anger, tension, and anxiety.

- *Perfectionism that has its roots in the child's temperament.* There is a class of children who do not need outside pressure to motivate their behavior. They have high expectations for themselves and are frequently critical of their own mistakes. I recall watching a seven year old reprimand herself for making small marks outside the printed line as she drew in a coloring book.

- *Chronic tension within family or social relationships.* We do not often think of burnout as it relates to our relationships with others. It is possible, though, that a child who is worn down by chronic arguing and broken communication patterns can experience a tense feeling that breaks his spirit. A preadolescent boy once remarked, "I've given up on myself. My mother and I have argued for so many years that I don't think we can ever get along. And it's been so long since my dad has given me a compliment that I'm not sure he knows how."

    The pace of the life–styles of many families is accelerated beyond the point of tolerance for children and teenagers. Many of these young people will complain later in life that they were cheated out of the elements that could have made their early years more satisfying. Rather than enjoy the experience of a well–ordered life with family and peers, the harried child may instead view life as a lost race against time that results in streams of tension and anxiety.

Managing the Anxious Child

Because anxiety is a disorder that involves fear, the parent feels an overwhelming urge to step in and take charge of the child's out–of–control emotions. This urge is based on the rationalization that the child is not able to harness his own anxiety and needs the support that can be offered by the stronger adult.

Effective management of anxiety recognizes the child's need for guidance through an emotional maze while at the same time allowing for the child's need to rely on his own inner resources. A healthy balance of providing guidance and allowing the anxious child to effectively confront his fears should be a goal of the parent.

The psalmist poetically encourages us to "Cast your cares on the Lord and He will sustain you" (Ps. 55:22). A job of parenthood is to provide the framework within which spiritual truths may be taught and eventually understood by the developing child.

The family of the anxious child plays a significant role in the successful control of this emotion. As important as it is to provide consistent behavioral boundaries to the child, it is more important to communicate to the child the steadfast belief that the world is a safe place and that the child's place in that world is secure. The child will more closely observe those nonverbal messages sent by the parent than the behavioral guidelines that are given.

Avoid increasing anxiety through overprotectiveness. It is a natural for parents to want to protect their children. This protective instinct is based on our unconditional love of our offspring and a genuine desire to assure that our children enjoy life and grow to become all they are capable of being. When the child is very young, he certainly needs the loving care of his parent, for without it he could not survive.

Perhaps one of the more difficult tasks of parenthood is in knowing when and how to allow the child to become more independent in making the decisions and choices that will eventually shape his adult life. In an effort to prevent a young person from making potentially devastating mistakes, an overprotective stance may be innocently taken. Even Jesus' mother had to guard against her parental inclination toward protecting her child (Luke 2:48). The child may become more fearful of his world because he has been kept too much from potential harm and does not know how to deal with life's inevitable stress. While a child's increased anxiety may pull many parents toward an even stronger protective stance over him, his actual need is for a greater degree of autonomy over the choices he must make.

—Case Study—

Throughout his childhood years Tom depended heavily upon his mother, particularly when faced with demands and pressures he felt inadequate to handle. He tended to look to his mother for answers to his problems. In fact, Mother did provide those sought–after solutions. Realizing her overprotective nature and its enhancement of Tom's tentative behavior, she determined to let the boy make more decisions on his own.

As Tom faced the prospect of taking a science test in school the following day, his confidence wavered noticeably. He sought out his mother, hoping for an answer to his problem. "Mom," he began, "I'm not feeling well. Would you check to see if I have a fever?"

Mother obliged. "No, Tom, I don't detect any fever. Tell me how you feel." As mother and son talked, Mother realized that her son wanted to avoid the next day's science test. He was hoping she would give him permission to do so.

Once the inevitable subject of school attendance came up, Mother quickly told Tom, "Even though you're not feeling well right now, you should still make plans to go to school tomorrow. I won't let you stay home because you are feeling ill over a science test."

"Well, if I fail that science test, it won't be all my fault! I *am* sick and I can't study so I know I won't be ready for that test tomorrow, and you're going to make me go anyway. I could stay home tomorrow, and you could call the school and tell them that I've been sick. You wouldn't be lying, and I might do better on the makeup exam." Tom hoped his appeal would strike a chord with his mother and encourage her to protect him from potential failure. His plan did not work.

"Tom, I understand how important it is to you to do well on tomorrow's test. I hope you are able to do your best." Having said that, Mother left Tom's presence and tended to her own activities.

Not one to give up so easily, Tom followed his mother and continued to plead for permission to miss school the following day. He threw in innuendos that his mother must not care for him and made the prediction that she would feel guilty when he brought home a poor grade.

Recognizing Tom's ploy to have her swoop him under her protective wing, Mother successfully sidestepped Tom's attempt to shift his fears to her. The following morning, Tom continued his anxious activity as he worked himself into an emotional frenzy before going to school. Mother remained firm throughout the ordeal. With reluctance Tom went to school and took his test.

That afternoon when Tom arrived home from school he told his mother he had passed the science test, although his grade was not as high as he had hoped for. Upon hearing the news, Mother stated, "Well, you passed. A higher grade would have made you happier, but I am glad you were able to take the test and do all right."

"I'm making a 'C' in science now. If I do better on the remaining tests, I can still make a 'B' for the semester." Tom was able now to put his school status in proper perspective.

Mother took advantage of Tom's subdued mood and added, "You know, Tom, last night you were quite worried about how you would do on the test and tried to talk me into allowing you to stay home from school. I was unwilling to argue with you over that issue. At the time, I didn't feel that you wanted to hear my arguments about why I thought you should attend school. You may have felt I was ignoring you but I wasn't. I simply realized that the best help I could offer you was to allow you to face your fears without my interference. I'm glad it worked out well."

"But, Mom, what if I had failed the test? Wouldn't you have felt guilty then?"

"No, I don't believe I would have. You could have learned from that experience as well. I think you can see that I'm committed to letting you learn to confront your fears on your own. I've decided that's the best way for you to develop greater confidence in yourself."

It is difficult for a parent to disengage from an overprotective pattern with a fearful child. Anxious children have a way of pulling at the heartstrings of their mothers or fathers. In the initial stages of developing an overprotective pattern of reacting to a child, the parent feels he is simply giving his child a little boost. But as this pattern continues, many parents feel that the child not only has grown dependent on the parent, but expects the parent to be completely responsible for alleviating the child's fears. A parent's effort to withdraw from this pattern may be made difficult by the child's resistance to such change.

Like Tom, most fearful children will show a heightened level of anxiety in an effort to continue to draw themselves under the protection of their parents. Tom's mother recognized his desire for this protection and sent him the message that she would not become entangled in an emotional struggle with him. She correctly waited until Tom's emotions were stable before explaining her strategy. Her honest expression about his emotional needs coupled with her belief in his ability to exhibit greater emotional control strengthened her leadership position as his parent.

There is the likelihood that Tom will continue to seek his mother's protection from his anxieties. However, her continued refusal to engage in power struggles with him will improve his ability to manage his own fears.

Communicate your faith in your child's ability to respond to his fears. The communication a parent has with his child is the most important component of a management plan aimed at shaping the child's behavior in a positive way. A child who feels understood by his parent is far more likely to accept the leadership of that adult than the child who feels alone with his thoughts and emotions.

A common tendency in trying to alleviate the anxiety of a child is to reason with him about how unnecessary his worry is. It is possible to use logic in explaining to the child why he should view the world more positively, yet still have a limited effect on his emotional status. Paul's counsel to "Carry each other's burdens" (Gal. 6:2) can certainly be extended to a parent's need to effectively communicate with a child struggling with anxiety. Several guidelines are offered to the parent who wishes to improve communication with a child struggling with his emotions:

- *Listening is the most important of all communication tools.* A parent who listens to his child momentarily steps out of his own world of thought and into the child's. Life is seen as the child sees it. Regardless of how illogical, impractical, or unreasonable the child's thoughts are, the parent who listens is trying to understand the child's communication in a complete way. Through this understanding, the parent can make decisions about the course of action that is needed on the child's behalf.

  A parent may practice the art of listening by observing his child in a variety of circumstances. During these observation periods, the parent should focus not only on the child's behavior, but upon the reasons the child has chosen to act, think, and speak as he has. A child of 3 years, 10 years, or 15 years will view the same situa-tion differently. The parent's ability to interpret the world from a vantage point different than his own is critical in the development of communication between parent and child.

- *Communicating to the child that he has been heard involves an ability to respond to him in a way that suggests understanding.* To an anxious child who is falling farther behind in school due to his lack of self–confidence a parent may respond, "I know you are disappointed in how things are going at school. It's times like these that make you want to simply give up." Such a reaction from the parent can cause the child to feel his parent is competent to help since he is capable of interpreting the child's own emotions correctly.

- *When confrontation is required from the parent, the child's emotional needs must be the foremost priority.* Confrontation is rarely effective when it comes from a parent who has not first shown the ability to listen and to understand the child. An anxious adolescent who is having difficulty in social relations with his peers may hear his parent say, "You are defeating yourself with your own behavior. Other teenagers would be more attracted to you if you would be more assertive." The parent is taking a risk in this bold statement. The effectiveness of such a remark will depend upon how well that teenager feels the parent knows him. It will be more completely absorbed by a young person who has a healthy communication pattern with his parent than by one who is convinced that his parent is speaking with little understanding of the teenager's needs.

- *Timing is a critical element.* There is little doubt that *what* is said to a child or adolescent about his behavior is not nearly as important as *when* it is said. Circumstances often dictate that the parent display leadership that requires unpopular decisions or actions to be made. Knowing that the child is wrapped up in his own emotional struggle, the parent may correctly choose to withhold further explanation or reasoning until a later time. For example, when a child is emotionally, or even physically clinging to his parent because of his fear of separation, it is not the time to convince him that he will have a good experience once he engages in the activity he now fears. His emotional intensity will not allow for such a prediction. Or, to one who is convinced that defeat of some kind is pending, an attempted pep talk may result in argumentativeness by a disbelieving child.

When the parent recognizes the child is filled with anxiety, it is generally best to say little, act decisively, and trust the child to learn from his experience. Guidance, opinions, or interpretations may be offered after the anxiety has subsided. Proper timing of statements allows the child to learn responsibility for his own emotional control and solidifies the parental position of leadership within the family.

Encourage relaxation as an alternative to anxiety. A child cannot be both tense and relaxed at the same time. The two states of being are opposite. Of those children who are anxious, few know how to genuinely relax. Teaching this skill to the child can offer him relief from the discomfort that accompanies anxiety.

Before discussing an approach to teaching relaxation to a child, it must be emphasized that the role model presented to the child by the parent is critical. As previously noted, children may learn many behaviors by observing the parent. The parent who displays a relaxed nature may be characterized by the following:

- Composed and controlled in situations that are emotion ladened.
- Decisive when called upon to make decisions.
- Not prone to wide mood swings.
- Organized but not to the point of compulsiveness.
- Generally optimistic that the child will move in a positive direction.
- Possessive of a good sense of humor.
- Interested in continually developing both mind and spirit.
- Willing to admit to mistakes and shortcomings.
- Open to alternative points of view.

I recognize that this list of characteristics represents an ideal to be sought. It is difficult for any parent to exhibit perfection in personal character. My point is that the tendency of the parent to display a relaxed nature increases his effectiveness in encouraging the same in a child.

To actively teach relaxation to an anxious child, the following suggestions are offered:

- At least 30 minutes before bedtime engage the entire family in a quiet activity.

- Spend from 10 to 20 minutes during this quiet time talking with the child. Discuss any topic of interest to the young person, letting him direct the flow of conversation.

- As the child or adolescent retires, have him take deep breaths. Tell him to pretend his arms and legs are so heavy they cannot be lifted. Have him imagine his limbs are completely limp. Spend a few minutes encouraging this calming approach to restfulness.

- Throughout the day when the child seems to be tense or has been excited, have him take a few minutes for a relaxation break. Encourage him to take similar breaks when he is away from home and finds himself under pressure.

- Avoid engaging in rough play, teasing, or other activities that may cause too much emotional arousal.

- Maintain a routine that is generally predictable.

Relaxation is a skill a child can learn both by observing his parent or through the direct intervention efforts of the parent. In a household that is relatively free from tension and chaos, it is easier for adults and children to flow more easily through the demands of each day. The relaxed parent has more emotional energy to give to his child. Similarly, the relaxed child has emotional energy to meet life's challenges.

Actively manage your child's stress. Children are not born with a natural inclination to manage their time efficiently. In fact, most children try to squeeze as much enjoyment as possible from a given amount of time. In my home, my wife and I frequently must tell our three daughters that their planned activities cannot be crammed into the time available to them. We have learned that to leave our children to their own scheduling devices would result in a time management nightmare.

When children and adolescents make plans to engage in an activity, they typically fail to consider all of the potential consequences of their choices. The parent must assume the leadership role of making decisions that can prevent the buildup of the level of stress that leads to childhood burnout. Of course, not all decisions made by the parent will be popular with the child. A responsibility of parenthood, however, is to make some decisions based on long–term positive effect on the child rather than on short–term popularity.

Ways parent can help manage the stress of a potentially harried schedule include:

- *Limit to three or four the number of outside activities in which the child is allowed to engage.* While there are many enjoyable and worthwhile activities available to children, participation in too many can put a damper on their usefulness to the child. It can also virtually ensure that other more important obligations will not be adequately met.

- *Limit the number of activities you, as a parent, are engaged in.* A child who frequently comes home to a weary parent (or to an empty house) can feel the negative effects of the parent's overworked schedule and may fail to be assured of his place of importance within the family structure. The overinvolved parent also serves as a negative example to the anxious child.

- *Maintain an organized household. It is emotionally settling for the child to experience a well–ordered life–style.* The security of a predictable schedule and orderly surroundings contrast with the frustration that can be produced by a hectic pace, unpredictable timetable, and cluttered environment.

- *Set aside at least 30 minutes at the end of each day to unwind.* A child who races through the day only to come to a screeching halt as he plops into bed at night fails to derive the benefit of a designated quiet time prior to the end of the day's activities. As the child grows older, he can be taught to use this time for reading, personal devotion, or conversation with other family members.

- *Place the family on a TV diet.* Overuse of the TV in our society contributes heavily to the lack of family togetherness experienced in many homes. Judicious use of this form of passive entertainment opens doors for other family oriented activities. As a family spends more time interacting with one another, children and teenagers find greater pleasure in their relationships with parents. The cooperative feeling within the family results in a relaxing impact upon the young person.

As a child grows into adolescence there are increasing demands on the teenager's schedule from sources outside the family. While balance must be maintained between overprotectiveness and permissiveness, the parent continues to bear a responsibility for overseeing the general direction of the young person's activities. While childhood burnout is common, this phenomenon is even more prevalent during the adolescent years as many youth engage in as many activities as possible. Parental guidance in stress management during these years can prevent a lifelong pattern of overcommitment that so frequently accompanies stress and anxiety.

Summary

Anxiety is an emotion that is often difficult to recognize in children because it can be masked in a variety of ways. It may fail to become a problem until several years of frustration have developed within the child. In many cases, parents are surprised to learn of the child's anxiety since, in a variety of ways, this child can be pleasant and cooperative. The condition of anxiety may be characterized by:

- A personalized reaction to the stressors of life.

- An exaggerated interpretation of normal situations.

- Increased demands for protection from others.

- Indecisiveness in order to avoid conflict with others.

- Difficulty engaging in activities separate from family or close friends.

- Exaggerated or increased complaints of physical discomfort.

While anxiety is often born out of the child's own emotional tendencies, it can be further heightened by the response others give to him. Circumstances that can influence increased childhood anxiety include:

- Too much pressure for the child to succeed.

- Guarding the child from potential misfortune through overprotection.

- The presence of adults who serve as role models for anxiety.

- Inborn inclination toward a sensitive nature.

- Power struggles designed to control fearfulness.
- The life–style of a demanding schedule.

Management of the anxious child involves a balance between too much parental intervention in the form of overinvolvement and a lack of parental leadership and assertiveness. Objective management of the child's emotions is critical. Management needs of the anxious child include:

- The parents' willingness to be consistent in placing behavioral limits on the child.
- Communication patterns that emphasize the child's self–importance and his ability to be autonomous.
- A life–style that encourages relaxation.
- Parental leadership that prevents an overcommitment to the demands of others.

Session 1

Study Session Objective:

To observe your child's reaction to stressful circumstances and understand the reasons for his reaction.

Biblical Reference: Matt. 6:25–34

Christ characterizes the qualities of an anxious person. He teaches that anxiety can be relieved through a life–style that relies on God's strength. Use your understanding of anxiety and your position as God's designated leader of the family to provide emotional comfort and stability to your child.

Discussion Questions:

1. How does your child typically communicate the emotion of fear? Through withdrawal? Increased hyperactivity? Complaints of illness? How good are you at recognizing the fear reactions of your child?

2. What sources of stress are present in your child's world? To what degree do you or other family members contribute to this stress? Does your child think you understand his world? How does he let you know?

3. In what ways does your child display indecisiveness? By putting off having to make decisions, what harm is he creating for himself? What is the result of this behavioral characteristic?

4. What physical symptoms does your child experience that appear to be related to anxiety? How does your child take advantage of these symptoms to alleviate his fears? Or, do his physical illnesses only make matters worse for him? In what ways?

5. How convincing is your child when he talks of the things that bother him? Do you also worry about many of the same things your child worries about? What effect does your own concern have on him?

Assignments:

1. Make a list of the things your child worries about. Identify those that you believe to be out of proportion. Then place yourself in your child's position for a moment and try to identify why he worries about these matters. You don't have to agree with his reasoning. Just understand it.

2. Begin to practice the art of communicating without words. When your child expresses a concern, refrain from trying to talk him out of that worry. Take note of your child's reaction. What did you learn?

Session 2

Study Session Objective:

To work toward eliminating those factors that contribute to your child's anxiety.

Biblical Reference: Phil. 4:5–9

Use the Apostle Paul's words to continue to develop a peace with yourself. As you practice a life–style marked by confident Christian living, your child will reap benefits.

Discussion Questions:

1. What stress is directly generated from within your family onto your child? How much control do you have over these circumstances? If you have little control, how can you influence your child's reaction to these problems?

2. In what ways does your child solicit protection from you over his worries? How does he use the protection others provide as a means of feeling a sense of personal power? How could this cause eventual harm in him?

3. Does your child know how to properly assert himself to others? Is he overextended in his activities? Do you feel guilty when you have to tell your child he cannot participate in an activity of his choice?

4. What type of atmosphere is present at home? Is there a "hurried" feeling? Do family members take time to communicate with one another?

Assignments:

1. Focus for several days on the timing of the statements you make to your child. When you feel justified in making a critical remark to him, stop and quickly assess the probable effect of your statement. If you think your child is not likely to accept what you have to say, wait for a better moment.

2. Examine the way you approach life. Identify at least 3–5 ways you can go about your daily routine in a more relaxed manner. Extend this more relaxed approach to your child's activities as well.

4

Woe Is Me—

The Depressed Child

JERRY COMPLAINED that he had few friends. He was convinced that whenever he was with other children they did not want him around. As a result he tended to keep to himself in order to prevent potential ridicule. The irony of his withdrawn nature was that by isolating himself, the other kids really did wonder what was wrong with him. Some of Jerry's peers were relatively friendly to him, while others scarcely knew when he was around.

At home Jerry showed a different set of behaviors. He still complained of feeling unwanted, but he lashed out at family members with unbridled anger in a manner not normally shown to others. The eruptions were not common, but were intense when they occurred. His mother and father knew of no way to control Jerry but to try to overpower him. At times they succeeded, but at other times it was evident that Jerry had the upper hand.

Much of Jerry's time was spent watching TV or sitting in the bedroom listening to his radio. Many times he sat alone in his room for long spans of time and did absolutely nothing. When asked to participate in activities, he usually refused in spite of previous frequent complaints of boredom.

One reason Jerry would give for not wanting to join in leisure activity was that he did not feel well. Though there was little cause to believe he was ill, he was forever complaining of a stomachache, headache, or similar ailment.

Jerry's parents did what they could to cheer their son up, but little seemed to work. He would not believe them when they said other children would play with him if he would only show some initiative. He pouted or became angry when they chastised him for his poor social behavior. He refused to listen when they tried to compliment him. His mom and dad knew something was wrong, but did not know how to help him.

Defining the Depressed Child

Depression is a term many Christians do not like to use, for to acknowledge depression suggests the failure to receive God's assurance of eternal love and personal acceptance. Christians are not spared from depression, though Christian faith can play a dominating role in overcoming its effects. The prophet Jeremiah suffered depression regarding the destruction of Jerusalem (Lam. 3:1–21). Jonah openly showed despondency following his contact with the people of Nineva (Jonah 4:3, 8). It is even likely that the boy Ishmael experienced depression along with his mother, Hagar, after they were expelled from Abraham's household due to Sarah's jealousy (Gen. 21:9–19).

Depression, it was once thought, was only possible in adulthood. Children were not felt to be able to experience an emotion as complex as depression. Yet the study of childhood behavior over the past generation has taught us that depression can be identified even in the very young child. As in the case of Jerry, a complicated mixture of symptoms can be blended into a pervasive pattern of depression.

Depression involves more than the periodic "blue" feeling that all young people experience. It is normal for children to have a bad day now and then. A depressed condition is more long-lasting. Dissatisfaction with oneself and with life in general goes on for weeks, months, and even years.

The course of depression varies. Many children may weave in and out of a depressed state. At times, the condition will run its course and the child will seem to be "himself" again. With little notice, the depression will return to wreak havoc on its victim. Other children are chronically depressed, reacting to one source of stress after another. To these sufferers, no other life–style is known.

Though statistics on childhood and adolescent depression are scarce, professionals agree that is a common condition. Data that are available show the suicide rate among adolescents to have steadily increased over the past 30 years. In fact, suicide is the second leading cause of death among teenagers, behind automobile accidents. (And there is considerable speculation that many single–car accidents are intentional suicide attempts by distressed youths.)

As we examine the definition of depression, it must be kept in mind that this is a complex condition. The symptoms that define it may vary in their intensity and duration. Not all young people display depressed feelings in the same manner. Nonetheless, many commonalities are seen in the behavior patterns of depressed children.

Interest in normal activities is lost. In listening to parents talk about a depressed child, I often hear the phrase, "My child just doesn't seem to care anymore." Actually, most depressed children and teens care quite strongly about their own negative emotional states. Their displays of apathy are an outgrowth of the sense of despair that so frequently accompanies this condition.

One 16–year–old young man told me, "I tell people that I feel OK inside, but I know I don't act like everything is OK. I guess I've learned to disguise the pain I feel. I really feel awful. But I don't expect things to improve anytime soon, so why should I try to improve myself? It won't do me any good."

The statement of this adolescent typifies the conflict that is so frequently a part of depression. Despite all the evidence that suggests apathy, much internal pain is not adequately expressed. The child feels alone in his struggle for greater satisfaction.

Listed on the following page are some of the ways a child or adolescent may display apathy that suggests deeper emotional discomfort:

- Remains isolated from a group due to feeling unaccepted.
- Displays restless behavior, but will not engage in an activity.
- Complains frequently, but does nothing to change the negative situation.
- Prefers to be alone much of the time.
- Shows little reaction to either positive or negative events.
- Refuses to develop skills and capabilities.
- Fails to utilize skills and capabilities that have been developed.
- Becomes involved in negative behavior that almost certainly will be discovered.
- Daydreams frequently.
- Fails to pursue potential relationships.
- Refuses to respond to requests for help or does so begrudgingly.
- Uses humor or sarcasm to mask true feelings.
- Openly questions the value of life.
- Holds steadfastly to a pessimistic view of the future.
- Brushes aside rules and considers them useless.

Apathetic behavior is a subtle way that children express feelings of internal stress. Since demonstrating a caring attitude has often resulted in emotional hurt, the young person builds a wall around himself to guard against the potential for further depression. A stated lack of interest in life's normal activities keeps the child from putting himself in a vulnerable position. However, the child loses sight of the reality that a lack of personal involvement with other people ensures that his dreaded depressed state will continue. Thus, the apathy that shields him from life's harm also perpetuates emotional discomfort.

Potential level of competence is not reached. The potential competence of a child is difficult to gauge. As parents, we often are guilty of overestimating the capabilities of our children. This flaw, however, is not altogether bad since it represents a desire for our children to do well in life.

When depression occurs, deterioration occurs in one or more areas of the child's activities. It is possible that a child will continue to do well in some aspects of his life, but may demonstrate a marked decline in other areas. Consider the following scenarios:

- A boy continues to do well in his classes at school, but declines drastically in his play on the baseball team. When playing baseball, he is listless, puts forth little effort, and makes only nominal attempts to contribute to the good of the team.

- A teenage girl maintains her active social schedule and always manages to look neat and well–groomed when she leaves the house. When at home, though, she places little emphasis on neatness. Unlike times past, she no longer cares how she looks at home nor shows concern for her belongings.

- Depressed about her relationships with her peers, a girl becomes reclusive and chooses to be with her parents rather than join in with other teenagers. Her behavior at home remains exemplary despite the withdrawal from her friends.

In each of these cases a deterioration in physical activity, family responsibility, or social functioning was present, even though the child's involvements in other areas remained rather high. In these cases, feelings of depression may be directly related to the circumstances of a given situation. Depression may be a reaction to difficulties experienced in one aspect of life, whether it be a lack of athletic success, a strain in family relations, or insufficient social confidence. Children who experience depression demonstrate a lack of competence and subsequent irresponsibility in a wide range of functions.

—Case Study—

Jenny is a junior–high–aged girl who has a better than average level of intelligence. Yet for years she has struggled to make passing grades in school. Her primary problem is simply not completing the work assigned to her. While at school she seldom interacts with others and keeps to herself most of the time. She complains of having no friends, although other children have made repeated attempts to include her in their activities.

When at home, Jenny rarely engages in social activity. She will at times play with a younger girl who lives nearby, but otherwise has no social interaction. She does only limited work around the house, and then does a poor job. She doesn't get along with family members and avoids having to discuss problems with them because of her fear of an argument.

In short, Jenny's entire life–style may be described as depressed. With little to encourage her in the form of success or positive relationships, she has become dissatisfied with life. She displays her despair through a life–style marked by little initiative and responsibility. Because of her depression, she falls far short of her full potential.

Personal value is not understood. It is my strong belief that every person has inherent value. Though man is sinful and fallen, he nevertheless still bears the image of God (Gen. 1:27; Gen. 9:6; Ps. 8:3–5; 1 Cor. 11:7). There is nothing an individual can do to add to this inherent value, though his choices to develop positive, godly behavior enable him to express that God–given value. Neither is there a behavior so bad that it detracts from someone's worth as a person. Each person dies with exactly the same amount of inherent value that he inherits on the day of his birth.

This concept is a spiritual truth we need to absorb. The first passages of Scripture inform us that man is the climax of God's creation (Gen. 1:27–31). Christ reminds His anxious listeners that the good of mankind is foremost in the thoughts of God (Matt. 6:30). The Creator of all things even places each of us on par with Himself when he calls us "friend" (John 15:14–15). Despite these evidences of an individual's value, children and teenagers may be uncertain that they have personal worth. Their experiences may have led them to an erroneous conclusion.

One way individuals separate themselves from one another is in the way they use the capabilities they have. One child may use his personal skills to become a master criminal whose life is marked by one misdeed after another. A second child may employ his given strengths to become a positive influence in his world, freely giving of himself to serve others.

The difference between these two young people lies less in their inherent goodness than in the *interpretation* of their value to others. In the first case, the child ignores the valuable contributions he is capable of making to his world and chooses to take advantage of others. In the second example, the individual recognizes his ability to give of himself to others and willingly does so.

While I did not use this analogy to suggest that depression results in criminal behavior, I would suggest that many children and adolescents fail to recognize the value they have as individuals. Consequently, they can develop a life–style that lacks a sense of fulfillment.

I have heard many depressed youths exclaim, "I am not an important person!" The method of expression may differ from child to child, but an overwhelming belief of the depressed child is that his value as an individual does not favorably compare to others. This misunderstanding of the value that is within him leads to a display of inadequacy. Ways in which a child or adolescent may display a perceived lack of worth include:

- Quitting a club or organization because of perceived insignificance. ("They'll never miss me.")

- Failing to extend aid to others for fear of being rejected. ("He doesn't want my help.")

- Resisting affection due to a feeling of unworthiness. ("She can't really love me.")

- Deliberately breaking rules thinking that to follow them will mean failure. ("Others expect too much of me.")

- Not recognizing that errors can be corrected. ("I'll never get it right.")

- Refusing to admit to a wrongdoing to save face. ("Why do I always lose?")

- Rejecting the need to learn. ("What difference will it make if I know that?")

- Unwillingness to share with others. ("I seldom receive anything good, so I'm going to hoard what I have.")

- Blaming others for setbacks. ("Others try to make my life difficult.")

- Rejecting of spiritual goals that provide direction to life. ("Surely God can't love me.")

An understanding of these outward displays reveals that depression encourages emotional immaturity within the young person. Because he lacks any comprehension of personal worth, the child is unable to extend himself to others, has difficulty relating to others emotionally, fails to utilize his skills, displays limited insight of behavior, and has limited direction in life. Thus, a part of the depressed condition involves a lack of understanding of what the child can contribute to himself and others simply because of his worth as an individual.

Expression of emotions is awkward. The ability to express feelings openly is one of the best tools for effectively coping with emotional distress. For the depressed child, the inability to communicate emotions brings on feelings of despair. Some children fail to communicate with others because they believe that if a problem is ignored, it will disappear. Others try to talk, only to experience the frustration of being misunderstood. As a defense against further exasperation, the child may withhold his emotions.

A child or adolescent can only withstand a given amount of suppressed emotional tension before depression sets in. If the emotion is not expressed in acceptable verbal communication, it will be displayed in other fashions. Following are examples of behavior patterns that represent disguised methods of communicating depressed feelings.

- Sixteen–year–old Shay is constantly at odds with her parents over petty matters. Her behavior includes expressions of rage and a desire for revenge for her parents' strict stance with her. While recklessly driving her car one day, a frightened friend tries to reason with her by saying, "Shay, slow down or you're going to wreck your car and we could be hurt!"

  Unmoved by her friend's plea, Shay laughs and says, "Boy, wouldn't my parents feel guilty about the fight we had this morning if I had a wreck and hurt myself this afternoon!"

Shay's inability to express herself honestly is manifested by the careless manner in which she handles herself behind the wheel of a car.

- Upset over the divorce of his parents, Jackie does not know how to tell others of his sadness. At age 13, he develops a habit of soiling his pants several times a week. When confronted with the evidence of his behavior, he routinely denies responsibility and becomes verbally abusive. Jackie's unusual expression of emotion simultaneously represents feelings of sadness over his parents' divorce, pleas for the kind of attention he received as a young child, and punishment of his parents for destroying a family.

- Twelve–year–old Hudson feels that his place in the family is overshadowed by his younger sister who seems to be a "star" at everything she does. Feeling both jealous and inadequate, Hudson frequently ruminates about the raw deal life has given him. One weekend the boy struggles internally about his feelings of inferiority. Deciding to do something about it, he goes outside where his father is doing yard work.

  "Dad," Hudson demands, "I'm going to trim the hedges and you're going to pay me $15 for doing it!"

  Dad, not wishing to be told what to do by his son, retorts, "Young man, you won't tell me what I'm to pay you. You can trim the hedges, but I'll decide whether or not you get paid and how much you will get paid. It is not your decision to make!"

  With that response, Hudson proceeds to throw a tantrum and display anger in a way uncharacteristic of him. Dad is left wondering what is troubling his son.

In each of these examples, a child chose to express emotions in a disguised manner. The irony of depression in young people is that feelings that so badly need expression are frequently displayed in a deceptive manner. Consequently, others misinterpret the child's behavior as defiance, indifference, or a lack of cooperation rather than a signal of depression.

Complaints of physical discomfort are common. The close connection between mind and body is both fascinating and complex.

The better we begin to understand this relationship, the more we learn about the way emotions affect how we feel physically.

We all have good days when it seems we can accomplish any desired task and bad days in which nothing goes as it should. It is likely that most of us find that on the good days when we are mentally alert we also feel good physically. Conversely, on the days we can't focus mentally, we aren't at our peak physically either.

When depression strikes a child, the chronic feelings of dullness are both emotional and physical. Since the child may not be able to express his feelings, he resorts to a less refined and more disguised manner of expression. He may also indicate feelings of emotional discomfort through a variety of physical complaints.

—Case Study—

At age eight, Tina was showing increased signs of chronic depressed feelings. She had always been a sensitive child. Unlike her two siblings, she was quite dependent on her parents for emotional security. Even in the third grade she found it hard to leave home to attend normal childhood activities. Tina made no secret of her lack of confidence and frequently commented that she did not feel as competent as other children.

Over the course of several months, Tina began to express an increasing number of complaints about her stomach. She seemed to have a stomachache most of the time, accompanied by periodic problems with nausea and constipation. Tina's parents made regular visits to the pediatrician's office for medical consultation and treatment. Being unable to find a medical cause for her repetitive ailments, the physician referred Tina to my office.

Evaluation found Tina was suffering from childhood depression with marked emphasis placed on her perceived feelings of inadequacy in comparison to others. The physical discomfort she experienced was an awkward expression of her lack of satisfaction in life. The attention she received due to her frequent illness satisfied an immediate need for assurance, but interfered with the development of a sense of personal competence. Thus, mired in a web of self–doubt, Tina continued in her pattern of depression without feeling sure she had the capacity to develop into a person of value to others. Her illnesses were a means of communicating the depression she felt within.

Risk–taking behavior is increased. I am convinced that the high incidence of juvenile crime, drug abuse, alcohol abuse, and other forms of dangerous risk–taking behaviors in today's youth is related to the high occurrence of childhood and adolescent depression. Children are taught at an early age that these behavior patterns are not healthy and should be avoided, and yet they persist.

I have interviewed many young people who were heavily involved in risk–taking behavior. Some youth engage in such activities because their self–centered thinking convinces them they are above the laws of society. But most youngsters enter into potentially dangerous behavior patterns because they experience a depression that convinces them that no risk of bodily, legal, or social harm can be worse than the load of emotional pain carried within. Consider the following statements made to me by young people who experienced chronic depressed moods:

- Regarding his increased tendency to inhale paint fumes as a cheap way to escape reality for a few moments, an 11–year–old boy stated, "I know you're not supposed to sniff paint. It kills brain cells. But I hate being in trouble all the time at home, at school—everywhere! Who cares if I kill a few brain cells? Nobody will know. I don't think anyone knows I exist!"

- Commenting on his parents' recently imposed driving restrictions, a teenage boy remarked, "I don't blame my parents for not letting me drive. They don't want me to wreck their car. I brought this punishment on myself. I'll admit, though, that as soon as I get to drive again, I'll still take chances. This may sound weird to you, but I'm not really afraid of having a wreck. Sometimes I think I deserve to have bad things happen to me."

- Even though a nine–year–old girl had been warned that her continued temper tantrums would result in punishment, she did not change her behavior. She said, "I can't help it. I hate the way I act! I get so upset, though, that it all comes out. I hate myself when I throw temper tantrums!"

- A six–year–old boy who had run in front of several cars expressed, "My mother cries when that happens. She holds me and she cries and tells me she loves me and doesn't want me to get hurt. Then she whips me."

- A girl who was involved in promiscuous sexual behavior cried as she confided, "I know what everybody says about me. Not many people think very highly of me. I don't like what they say, but they're probably right."

Each of these children willfully displayed risky behavior as an outgrowth of depression even though they were fully aware that such behavior would bring about negative comments, criticism, punishment, or restrictions. The behavior pattern of children like these represents an awkward and often desperate attempt to convey the message, "I feel bad inside. Someone please notice and help me feel better about myself." But all too often, the child's behavioral pleas result in reactions that create further depression rather than provide emotional relief.

Life's purpose and meaning is evasive. Depression is frequently accompanied by an empty feeling. Although younger children cannot grasp the full meaning of the void within them, they intuitively know something is wrong. Adolescents can more accurately identify the lack of direction depression brings, but a clear description of feelings is still difficult.

Many times teenagers or pre–teens will show me poems or other samples of their written expressions. I am often struck by the sense of despair that is so common in these writings. The past is often described as "cruel," "lost," "a nightmare," or "a blank." The future is looked upon as "hopeless," "full of hurt," "confusing," or "just there."

A major goal of childhood is for the young person to enter adulthood with a solid understanding of who he is as a person, what his personal strengths and weaknesses are, and how he will use his assets to live a productive and satisfying life. Depression and its often–present negative pattern of thinking may not only encourage a child to feel insignificant compared to others, but also will cause a child to grow into an adult who fails to recognize his value as a spiritual being. This failure to identify the special place of mankind in a spiritual sense dooms the individual to dwell on his shortcomings.

Many parents purposely avoid attempts to influence their child's religious or spiritual beliefs. The argument is generally based on the assumption that when the child is older he will be capable of making sense of this aspect of life without interference.

—Case Study—

Heather was a college freshman who sought counseling through my office. During her first few sessions, she had difficulty expressing her need for guidance. She felt emotionally uncomfortable and hoped someone could soothe the restless feeling she continually experienced. As time passed, Heather talked of how many of her college friends seemed to have a stronger grasp on life than she did.

She told me, "A lot of people already know what they want to study in college and what occupation they want to pursue. I tell people I want to be a lawyer, but I only say that because my father is a lawyer. I am also asked what religion I am and I don't know what to say. I usually say I'm Baptist since we're in the Bible Belt, but I'm really nothing. I don't know anything about religion. I don't have any beliefs at all. I have no idea why I even exist."

Heather continued, "My parents have always told me they didn't want to push me to make decisions about my religious beliefs. They wanted me to decide for myself what I chose to believe. Now that I'm 18 years old, I don't know what to believe. One set of beliefs is the same as another to me. I'm an honor student, and I don't even know the difference between a Hare Krishna and a Catholic. Why did my parents do this to me?"

Heather's initial lack of direction during the early stages of counseling mirrored her lack of direction in life. She was eventually able to identify within herself depressed feelings that had roots in a spiritual void during her childhood development. This emptiness accompanied her into adulthood with no understanding of where she fit in the grand scheme of life itself. In her own correct way of thinking, she had not been done a favor, but was actually pushed toward feelings of aimlessness and despair.

Factors Influencing the Depressed Child's Behavior

Stress reactions may promote depression. In most cases, children experience depression as a reaction to stressful events or circumstances in their lives. Some sources of stress involve factors parents can control. Other sources of stress are outside the realm of the family and cannot be easily removed. Even so, the family can have an impact on the way the child or adolescent responds to that stress.

Many depressed children and teenagers experience depression as a result of relationship difficulties. One of the strongest needs for a child is to feel that he belongs and is a part of his family and social group. Interference in the development of relationships with others creates a major source of stress for the child and can propel the onset of depression.

Depression can also result from a traumatic incident. In such cases, the depressed feelings are usually short–lived and the child will soon return to his normal ways. Stressful occurrences of this nature include the following situations:

- Making a failing grade in school.
- Being overlooked for a desired position.
- Performing poorly in an organized activity.
- Failing to find someone to play with or go out with.
- Receiving a reprimand or punishment for a wrongdoing.
- Arguing with a family member or friend.
- Losing a favorite object, or even a pet.
- Having a request refused.
- Entering puberty.
- Moving from one place to another.

Each of these stressful matters may cause a minor setback to the child, but the harm will not likely be devastating. In fact, life without a certain amount of discomfort can actually inhibit personal growth. When children lack any kind of personal struggle, they may not learn to look within themselves and discover their inner strengths.

But when children experience lasting depression as a result of ongoing difficult circumstances, they may face a level of stress that makes coping difficult. Reducing the depression that causes such stress is difficult, yet, changes *can* be made. Examples of ongoing circumstances that can encourage depression in children include:

- Chronic arguing between family members.

- Marital problems between a child's parents.

- Lack of communication with a child on a one–to–one basis.

- Frequent criticism of a child.

- Infrequent displays of affection and positive attention.

- Misuse of family finances.

- Periodic substance abuse within the family.

- Inadequate parental control over the child's behavior.

- Limited social or intellectual stimulation.

- Persistent difficulties in getting along with peers.

- Perennial failure in school due to learning problems.

Each of these circumstances can have a marked negative effect on a child resulting in depression. These sources of stress cannot simply be ignored. As time passes, the child's emotional development only becomes more complex.

Sometimes children experience depression largely as a result of one major stressful event in their life, but the impact of the event may cause other less stressful circumstances to be magnified. Examples of events that can have a more severe impact on a child's emotional development include:

- Divorce of parents.

- Death of a loved one.

- Severe conflict among family members.
- An unwanted teenage pregnancy.
- Sexual molestation or abuse.
- A debilitating injury.
- Involvement with law enforcement officials.
- Severe substance abuse or alcoholism in the family.
- A suicide attempt by a family member.

These sources of stress have a severe impact on a child because of the irreversible damage that is inflicted. The stressful event cannot be removed from the child's past. Rather, emphasis must be placed on helping the child cope with the reality of what has happened and develop a new direction that will introduce a sense of hope for his or her future.

Predisposition toward depression. Some children have personality styles that make them more prone to depression. The major components of the personality of the sensitive child, for example, lend themselves to the development of depression. These characteristics include excessive sensitivity to the way others react, lack of assertive behavior, poor self–image, and a tendency to hide feelings in socially inappropriate ways. A child with a highly sensitive personality may develop depression when another child would simply take matters in stride and experience no emotional bruises.

The inclination of some children to develop depression coupled with their unavoidable life circumstances may result in chronic feelings of despair. With no control over his own inborn personality traits nor over other factors of life, a child can develop a pattern of persistent frustration. As unfair as it seems, the young person must bear the brunt of the responses others give to him.

—Case Study—

Susan, age 11, was brought to my office by her concerned parents at the suggestion of her school principal. Now in the sixth grade, Susan had failed two classes and was barely passing several others. Her parents, Mr. and Mrs. Little, had noted a steady decline in her school performance over the previous two years. However, her grades had never been as low as her most recent ones. Mr.and Mrs. Little were rightfully worried about Susan and wanted answers about their daughter's confusing pattern of behavior.

Evaluation of Susan found her to have a high I.Q., but also revealed the presence of a learning disability. Previously able to do well in school because of her superior intelligence, she could no longer compensate for her learning disabled condition. The result was poor grades.

The discovery of Susan's learning disability brought relief to Mr. and Mrs. Little since they knew her school problems were not a result of defiance or irresponsibility. Then they began to focus their concern on the effect of this disability on Susan's emotional makeup. Because she had done poorly in school, Susan had begun to see herself as "dumb" even though she was clearly quite intelligent. The frequent criticism and punishment by her parents had also encouraged her to feel rejected and misunderstood.

Susan's pattern of depression stemmed from a condition beyond her control—a learning disability. Several years of not recognizing this condition caused her to be vulnerable to a depressed emotional state.

Just as a learning disability can make a child question her worth as a person, so too can other physical circumstances promote depression. A clinically hyperactive child, for example, may receive more than his share of negativism from others, leading to a depressed mood. A child with a physical handicap may feel sufficiently different, resulting in despair. A child who lacks size, coordination, strength, or ability may be predisposed to depression because of his perceived difference from others.

While outside interferences quite often accompany depression, other characteristics that are beyond a child's control (personality traits, limitations in ability, physical attributes) can play a major role in the child's emotional state. The unique qualities of each child should not be overlooked as a potential factor in his emotional development.

Depressed feelings can be reinforced. It is often difficult to identify how certain behavior patterns are reinforced. Few parents intentionally set out to create depression in their child. Yet, the parent might unwittingly use habitual responses that encourage the formation of depressed symptoms in the young person. By visualizing the world from the child's point of view, the parent can better understand how various reactions may affect the child. It is the child's perception of his place in the world that determines his response to a situation, not the intention of others.

—Case Study—

Nine–year–old Jerrod sat quietly in his room, refusing to communicate with anyone else in the household. Thirty minutes earlier he had been involved in an altercation with his father that left him emotionally bruised.

On his day off, Dad had decided to repair a leak in the dishwasher. At one point, it had been difficult for him to leave his position to get a needed tool. Since Jerrod was nearby, he called upon the boy for help.

"Jerrod, go get me a Phillip's head screwdriver and be quick. I need it right now!" There was sternness in Dad's voice.

Jerrod was busy playing with a toy. He heard his father's request, but was internally offended by his father's forcefulness. Silently, Jerrod grumbled that his Dad could have been more polite in asking him to get the screwdriver. Slowly, he began to search for the tool.

"Jerrod! Why do you have to take so long? I can't even ask you to get a screwdriver for me without having to fuss at you. You know where I keep my tools in the pantry. Go do what I asked—now!"

Again, Jerrod gave little response other than to drag himself to the pantry and slowly search for a screwdriver. He thought to himself, "I hope there's not one in here. Then Dad could really have something to get mad about."

Growing increasingly impatient, Dad finally abandoned hope that his son would be of assistance. Getting up from the awkward position he was in, he found Jerrod standing in the pantry. His angry words brushed the youngster aside. "Forget it, Jerrod. I'll get it myself. I don't know why you can't be more responsible. You're old enough now that I should be able to count on you to help me, but you never seem to get it right." With a scowl on his face, Dad left behind his dejected son who then withdrew to his bedroom.

While by himself, Jerrod focused on his negative qualities. Various thoughts ran through his head, such as, "I can't do anything right;" "I never do anything to satisfy Dad;" "Everybody thinks I'm dumb;" and "I wish I could run away from all this."

While a single incident of this type will not result in a lasting depression, repeated situations in which a child feels belittled can reinforce his negative self–concept and lead to chronic feelings of inadequacy.

A depression–prone child can interpret other reactions as a reinforcement of his negative value. These include:

- Frequent criticism, even if the criticism is meant to be helpful. ("I can't do anything right.")

- Lack of time spent with the child on an individual basis. ("I'm not important.")

- Use of emotional intensity in communication. ("I cause others to feel upset.")

- Ignoring accomplishments and achievements. ("The things I do must not be good.")

- Providing attention primarily when bad things happen. ("I must be bad since that's what everyone seems to expect from me.")

- Inconsistency in following through with promises.`("Nobody cares if I become discouraged.")

A child continually assimilates the reactions he receives from others. Over the course of time a steady stream of negative circumstances contributes to feelings of low self–worth, which lead to chronically depressed feelings.

Researchers have coined the term "learned helplessness" to describe the reaction individuals have when they find themselves in a negative situation that offers little hope for relief. Faced with persistent defeat, the child may choose to give in to his hopeless circumstance. Punitive or critical reactions from others that are intended to spark change have the unintentional effect of encouraging a depressed spiral.

Depressed behavior may be imitated. Numerous factors contribute to the atmosphere of any home. Many of these components are mentioned in the introductory chapter of this book. In my opinion, the most important factor that determines the tone of the household is how the parents feel about themselves. Children are astute and quite adept at recognizing parental qualities that support or detract from the creation of a positive home environment. A child's recognition that his mother or father battles depression can spawn a similar struggle in his own emotional development.

—Case Study—

Leigh Ann was a distraught mother seeking assistance for her two daughters, both of whom were developing increasingly strong patterns of childhood depression. She explained that she recognized many of the subtle symptoms of this condition because she had experienced similar feelings as a child and, in fact, continued to battle this disorder. She told me, "Knowing the pain I went through as a child and the pain I still feel, it has always been my goal to try to provide the kind of life for my daughters I never had. I give them everything I can, but it doesn't seem to be enough. I can tell my girls are not happy." Leigh Ann talked with concern about her family.

She wanted to discover how she contributed to the depressed mood of her daughters, so we examined the atmosphere that was prevalent in her home. Soon she had named several ways she modeled her own depression to her children:

- Most mornings began with virtually no conversation among family members.

- Social activities were infrequent.

- Feelings of fatigue were persistent.

- Responsibilities that Mom could not fulfill were handed down to the girls.

- Good moods of family members were rare.

- Requests for attention were not often acknowledged.

- The children were often left to entertain themselves.

With dismay, Leigh Ann expressed guilt over her role in the incomplete emotional development of her daughters. She felt it was her fault that her children were cultivating the very symptoms she had hoped they could avoid.

With counseling, Leigh Ann was able to get beyond her feelings of guilt and create an opportunity to influence her daughters positively. She realized that the elements contributing to her negative home environment were under her control. She reasoned, correctly, that by consciously improving *her* behavior pattern, the model she presented to her daughters would in turn help them reverse their own negative moods.

Much of what children learn is by watching those who play a significant role in their lives. A vital factor in the development of a condition like childhood depression is the parents' own feelings about themselves. By imitating the parent and other significant role models, the child learns to experience similar emotions. He can become conditioned to react to the environment in the same way as his model.

Managing the Depressed Child

It is good that children are as emotionally resilient as they are. A child has the capacity to change his way of thinking in a way that an adult does not. Almost all depressed children hope that life will improve. Deep within the child is an element of optimism that believes life will soon be better.

One of the greatest sources of a child's despair is his heavy emotional dependence on others for stability and security. Yet that very dependency means that parents can make adjustments in their management of a depressed child and strongly increase the probability of a healthy change.

As in dealing with any behavioral or emotional problem, it is necessary to view the world from the eyes of a child. A clear

understanding of his interpretation of life marks the first step in
effectively managing his depression. Outlined in the following
pages are the major components of an effective management plan
for the depressed child.

Identify and eliminate as many sources of stress as possible.
You can't, or course, eliminate *all* stress factors in a child's life.
Don't feel badly that you can't. A child who glides through childhood
without experiencing at least a certain amount of discomfort will
be ill–equipped for adulthood. Your child will eventually meet face
to face with adversity and needs to know how to handle it.

However, a depressed child accumulates stress—creating
an emotional weight that causes him to stumble and plod through
life. It is this excessive stress which should be eliminated.

Be aware of two types of stress. The first type is stress over
which the family has some control. The second category is stress
that cannot be controlled.

The most common forms of depression are associated with
chronic stressful circumstances that combine to overwhelm the
child. Many of these factors were previously mentioned as influences on childhood depression, such as chronic arguing, family or
marital disorder, insensitive communication, and the like. Most of
these circumstances can be controlled.

The parent must recognize his role of leadership in the
home and its accompanying responsibilities. A parent who bears
the task of establishing a healthy home environment encourages
emotional growth.

Here are some goals parents can set to begin to alleviate the
effects of stressful events:

- A willingness to allow all members to have a voice in matters
  that affect the family.

- Showing a healthy respect for the child's opinion.

- Parental role models who are genuine and openly expressive.

- A schedule that is neither overly organized nor too chaotic.

- Healthy expressions of affection among family members.

- Recognition and appreciation of the unique qualities of individual family members.

- Flexibility to change as the situation requires.

- Demonstration of a good sense of humor.

- A patient attitude toward the mistake–prone child.

- Emotional control during times of distress.

Although it is difficult to quantify and measure these characteristics, the first step toward emotional well–being is an atmosphere free from lingering feelings of stress and tension. An environment that recognizes the child's emotional needs helps him see himself in a positive manner and develop healthy expectations of himself.

But what can parents do about the second category of stress and its circumstances they cannot control (such things as death, divorce, irreversible physical damage, and relationship difficulties outside the control of the family)? While parents may not be able to control the *existence* of these events, they can control their *response* in regard to the child. Controlled responses to unavoidable traumas can still have a powerful effect to diminish the amount of stress on the child. Guidelines for minimizing the effects of unforeseen sources of stress on the young person are as follows:

- Never ignore the reality of the effects of an event on the child.

- Don't hide information when it is certain that the child is likely to know about it.

- Refrain from developing an overprotective stance that diminishes the child's ability to learn responsibility.

- Avoid giving details that are not essential.

- Keep the child out of the middle of avoidable controversies.

- Maintain an open line of communication with the child.

- Allow the child to freely express his opinions and feelings, even if they are negative.

- Make more time than usual for conversation with your child.

- Approach your child and offer your undivided attention; don't wait for him to voice his need to be heard.

- Be patient when your child needs time to adjust to the change created.

- Maintain a life–style that is as normal as possible.

- Recognize the child's need to talk about his trauma even long after the event has passed.

A primary goal in dealing with the unavoidable traumas of life is to keep the child from inappropriately ignoring their effects on him. When parents show genuine concern, openness, effective emotional control, and simple patience, they can significantly minimize the effects of stressful circumstances and subsequent chronic depression.

Help reconstruct the child's self–esteem. As we have noted, depression creates a negative expectation by the child. He is unable to comprehend his value as a creation of God. The parent must be made to pass along this feeling of worth. The parent must remember this when the child feels incapable of completing an easy job or shows apathy when offered the opportunity to participate in an activity.

Don't even give a depressed child the opportunity to turn away from a potentially reinforcing encounter with others. For example, an apathetic child will quickly say no if asked if he would like to do something fun.

So rather than provide him an opening to reject the opportunity, the parent should simply get him involved without prompting, and follow up with a verbal reward. As this procedure is repeated, over time, a depressed child will recognize that others expect positive things from him and learn that he is a person others see as having value.

—Case Study—

Roy's parents came to my office out of concern for their 14–year–old son's growing dislike for himself. Recognizing that he suffered from low self-esteem, Mr. and Mrs. Fordham wanted to know how to better provide for Roy's emotional needs.

They knew they needed to emphasize Roy's capabilities, and they agreed to look for opportunities to demonstrate their belief that Roy was a competent person. I cautioned them not to feel discouraged if Roy was slow to respond. I also advised them to reward positive behaviors to help rebuild Roy's confidence step by step.

At our next meeting, Mr. and Mrs. Fordham reported improvement in Roy's behavior and responsibility. They said they had verbally reinforced Roy for improved behavior such as putting his socks in the laundry hamper, turning down the volume of his stereo when requested, and coming home before supper without a fuss. On one occasion, Mr. Fordham asked Roy to help lift a heavy object and followed the task with playful banter in which he told Roy he was glad to have an increasingly strong young man around the house.

Not only had Roy benefited from the increased positive attention given him, but also had his parents. As Roy responded to their reinforcement of his worth as a person, they found it easier to offer additional doses of their approval. Though Mr. Fordham had felt awkward engaging in a playful exchange with Roy, he recognized its positive effect on the adolescent.

When trying to reverse a trend of negativism in a child who is fighting depressed feelings, it is important for the parent to maintain leadership. A sense of confident resolve must support the parent's effort to redirect the child's opinion of his value. These guidelines are offered to help parents instill a greater concern for self in the depressed child:

- Focus on any small accomplishment, positive behavior, or improvement by the child.

- Engage the child in activities or interaction certain to be successful, followed by positive acknowledgement.

- Don't give up if the child is not enthusiastic. He is being cautious.

- Do not require excitement on the part of the child.

- Refrain from giving the child the opportunity to say no to a question. Make statements instead.

- Acknowledge the positive aspect of the child's behavior very frequently during the initial stages of building self–esteem.

A depressed child will not rid himself of this condition, nor will change come about immediately. The decision to focus on a child's positive nature requires a long–term commitment by the parents.

Stop the child's cycle of self–damaging behaviors. A common fault of the depressed child is acting in ways that strengthen his depressed feelings. Thinking that others do not care to be around him, he does things in ways to confirm his suspicions. He has a tendency to make statements such as, "I am dumb," "Nobody wants to do anything with me," or, "It doesn't matter what I think since I'm a nobody."

If not careful, the parent can unwittingly *encourage* the child's self–damaging behavior by offering assurance immediately following the youngster's negative expression. For example, a child may call himself "dumb" following a bad experience. A concerned parent may respond reassuringly, "You're not dumb. I think you're real smart. No one who is dumb can do all the good things you can do."

Though the intent of the parent's words is to cheer up an unhappy young person, the child may feel rewarded for the negative statement he made about himself. Many depressed children have learned that adults give them attention following a display of helplessness. Though a positive response is intended to dispel the child's negative self–image, the child may learn to use negative communication or behavior as a way to solicit attention.

An astute parent will make a mental note of a child's negative statement, recognizing the child's need for reassurance. He will pick a time, though, in which the reinforcement is not directly connected to a specific event so the child can appreciate the independent nature of the verbal compliment.

—Case Study—

Marjorie had experienced a particularly difficult day. Things had not gone well when she and a friend got together to play. Their time together was marked by one conflict after another, and Marjorie had been hurt by some of her friend's angry words.

Marjorie also had difficulties within her family. She and her brother had argued over petty matters throughout the evening. Her mother had scolded her for the irresponsible way she had been keeping her room. She and her father had a disagreement over the style of earrings Marjorie wanted to wear. In short, Marjorie's relationships with others that day had been strained. To express the frustration she had within herself, she made numerous derogatory remarks about herself, blaming herself for the day's troubles.

Marjorie's mother was the one to whom Marjorie directed most of her comments. Mom wanted to give her daughter immediate reassurance that she was not the negative person she felt herself to be, but she refrained because she knew that the timing was not appropriate for verbal encouragement. She did, however, make a mental note to herself to consciously look for opportunities to affirm her daughter.

Later that evening Marjorie's mood had softened somewhat. Mom noticed that she had made a little headway in cleaning her room, and thanked her. Marjorie didn't respond.

At bedtime, Mom made time to spend a few minutes sitting on the edge of Marjorie's bed and talk informally. Nothing important was said, but Marjorie seemed to appreciate of her mother's effort.

The next day Mom continued to look for opportunities that would help Marjorie see the positive aspects of her personality. She told her that her hair looked nice and commented on how her neatly made bed caused the bedroom to look more attractive. Other similar efforts were made to focus on the good things about Marjorie. As a result, Marjorie experienced a better day.

In addition to giving more positive comments to a child experiencing depression, it is also vital to consider the *timing* of such comments. Verbal reinforcement should follow a positive act or take place independent of an expression of negativism. Since reinforcement increases the likelihood that the behavior immediately preceding it will be repeated, a child's statements of inadequacy should be met with parental understanding coupled with a neutral reaction. But the parent should plan to show positive attention to alleviate the child's discomfort at an appropriate time in the future.

Make your positive comments count. Many frustrated parents tell me, "I try to be positive with my child, but it doesn't seem to work. Instead of responding favorably, my child finds a way to reject my effort to make him feel better."

Since depressed children and teenagers have such low self–esteem, it is important to understand how they interpret positive statements from others. A defeated child who hears himself described as "great," "wonderful," or "important" may reject such flowery adjectives. His self–concept will not allow him to view himself as great, wonderful, or important. He may see himself as inept, terrible, or insignificant.

Parent's Response
Child's Reaction
"See how smart you are?"
I'm not as smart as she thinks I am.
"It must feel good to have completed your homework."
It does *feel good. Maybe I'm smarter than I thought.*

Similarly, a depressed child who is referred to as a "hero," "angel," or "brain" may dismiss these descriptions as frivolous and unfounded. In his own mind he may feel that he is a goat, a no–good, or a dunce. So it is important that the words chosen by the parent to build up a child's failing sense of importance are realistic enough to be accepted by the child. Here are some examples:

- A child has just completed a simple homework assignment. Rather than tell him, "You've finished that with ease. See how smart you are?" the parent may state, "You've finished your assignment. It must feel good to be done." The first response could cause the child to question the parent's judgment since he does not see himself as a smart person. But he can readily agree that it feels good to be done with an assignment.

- Even though a young girl was not excited about having to fold clothes and put them away, she completed the unpleasant task. Her mother thanked her and added, "I'm glad you helped me put away the clothes. We won't have to do any more laundry for the rest of the week." The daughter is capable of deducting that her help was valuable. She can easily relate to her mother's satisfaction of having completed a week's worth of laundry.

- A teenager comes home from a date on time, a fairly rare occurrence. To refer to the adolescent as being dependable may not fit with his own assessment of himself. However, he can appreciate a statement such as, "Thanks for being on time last night because I like to know you are safely home." The teenager is then more likely to experience a positive reaction knowing that his cooperation helped his parent feel secure.

- A boy may reject a reference to him as "mother's big helper" because he is fully aware that on numerous occasions recently he has been less than helpful. He will more willingly accept an acknowledgement such as, "Your help on this job has made it much easier for me." He can then draw his own conclusion that he is capable of being a big help to his mother.

I certainly do not oppose the use of colorful, positive words and phrases as we talk to our children. A child wants and needs to know that his parent holds him in high regard even though the young person may have a low self–image. Yet for a depressed child to improve that self–image, the parent's statements must be both positive and factual. Arming the child with evidence of his worth gives him a reason to think more highly of himself. A child with a positive self–concept is far more likely to rid himself of the weighty emotional burdens that encourage depressed feelings.

Be spontaneous in giving rewards. A common practice in helping a depressed child feel more positive is to offer a valued reward at a designated time for positive behavior or performance. For example, a child may be offered his own telephone if he can maintain good grades for six weeks. He may be promised a meal at his favorite pizza restaurant if he refrains from emotional outbursts for only one week. The parent may strike any number of deals with a child to try to motivate him to a higher level of responsibility.

Often the child fails to reach the agreed–upon goal. Parents are left wondering what it must take to create a feeling of motivation within their lackadaisical child. Just when the parent thinks he has found the perfect incentive for his child, the young person loses interest in the promised reward.

Just as a parent must choose appropriate verbal rewards to build the child's self–image, he must also provide incentives that cause the child to realize that he is capable of experiencing success. In essence, the parent must see to it that the child or adolescent is "set up" for a reward.

For the difficult–to–motivate child who has little belief in himself, I suggest that the parent give unannounced rewards when the child doesn't expect it. The spontaneous nature of the reward has a strong effect and causes the child to want to repeat whatever it was that brought about the pleasant parental response. It also causes the child to view himself more positively since he has not once again spoiled a chance to earn something he really wanted. His faith in himself is not lost, but rather is made stronger.

—Case Study—

None of the incentives Dad tried with Jamie had worked. The 13–year–old boy remained unconcerned about his grades despite the very real possibility that he may fail the eighth grade. At various times during the school year, Jamie had been promised a new stereo, his own telephone, and a motorcycle as rewards for improved grades. He had seemed excited about the promise of each reward, but nothing had worked to bring up his grades. In addition, Jamie's parents had taken away many privileges, hoping that he would work harder to regain them. Yet Jamie's irresponsibility continued.

Willing to try a different strategy, Jamie's parents abandoned their efforts to coerce improvement with the offer of a reward. They were advised to keep closer contact with his teachers, who agreed to cooperate with their new plan. This called for the school counselor to send a message to Jamie's father or mother whenever he had experienced a good day at school.

A surprised Jamie was met by his dad one evening. Dad said, "Mrs. Young called today and told me she had checked with your teachers to see how you were doing. All but one told her you had completed most of your classwork. Mrs. Young felt this was an improvement and I agreed. Why don't we go out for hamburgers tonight? You choose where we will go."

Jamie was relieved at the good news and pleased to be rewarded for his improved effort in school that day. It was gratifying to be rewarded for his small accomplishment rather than criticized for his failures.

A continued effort was made to identify Jamie's small victories. With increased regularity, he was spontaneously rewarded for his improvement. The rewards were not always big. At times positive achievement was met with a compliment, a handshake, or a hug. On other occasions Jamie was surprised with a five–dollar bill, a later bedtime, or flexibility on some of his household chores. When Jamie's report card showed improvement, Dad rewarded him by completing Jamie's chore of taking out the garbage for a week.

As parents create opportunities for success, a depressed and unmotivated child can begin to see himself as capable of changing in a positive way. The effects of unannounced rewards are stronger than promised incentives. The child has been caught being good. He is not given the chance to talk himself into believing that a promised prize is not attainable. A cycle of positive expectations begins to replace the downward spiral of self–defeating behavior.

Allow the depressed child to talk freely. When a depressed child or adolescent first enters my office, it is frequently difficult for him to express how he really feels about himself. As the child begins to feel safe within the confines of the counseling office, his words flow more freely. It is common for the youth to state how relieved he feels simply as a result of the verbal outpouring of pent–up feelings.

The parent of a child grappling with depression is in a prime position to offer that child the opportunity to express his innermost thoughts and emotions. The parent should take leadership by approaching the child and showing a willingness to enter his world of thoughts. A child or teenager who is told, "You can talk to me anytime you need to," will usually find a reason to avoid dialogue. He may not want to burden his parents with problems that may sound insignificant to them. He may fear they will not be interested. Or he may not know how to bring up a subject of concern for discussion. The parent who makes himself accessible to his child will find that the informal talks he has with his child can open doors to more serious discussions.

When the child does begin to talk about his feelings, several important guidelines should be followed:

- The child's point of view should be understood. His interpretation of matters is important since his beliefs will largely determine future behavior.

- The nonverbal expressions of the parents should indicate a genuine interest in what the child is saying. Parental interest encourages increased dialogue.

- Questions should be presented as a way of gathering further information and not as a way of implying wrongdoing or guilt.

- Opinions, facts, or advice should be withheld when it is obvious that the child is not ready for such guidance.

- Emotional control by the parent will help the child maintain his own sense of composure. Lack of restraint will lead to a power struggle.

- The appropriate use of silence can allow the child to organize further thoughts that need expression.

- Emphasis on the feelings that underlie a child's statements are far more important than the words he speaks.

- Decisions that are made in haste may prove to be ineffective. Allow time to pass, if necessary, so decisions are well planned.

- Allow for disagreement. It is inevitable.

- Use confrontation only after the child feels he is understood. Let your confrontation be helpful rather than a weapon to be used in an attack of a child.

- Demonstrate respect through a warm tone of voice, receptive posture, and appropriate gestures.

As the young person verbalizes his feelings, he develops a greater capacity to accept responsibility for his own personal growth. As he talks, he can begin to recognize the feelings of anger, embarrassment, and fear that dominate his behavior. The guidance of the parents takes on greater value as communication improves.

I received a letter once from a young adult I had counseled when she was a teenager. In her letter she thanked me for the support and help she had been given through the counseling sessions we had. As I reflected on the time I spent with this young person, I recalled that I had not actually given her a lot of direct instruction. My role had been to listen to her, clarify her thoughts, and demonstrate faith in her ability to effectively confront difficult circumstances.

Children and teenagers come to understand themselves on the basis of the interactions they have with significant individuals in their lives. Parents who are willing to listen to a struggling child can become a major component of positive change.

Show your child that life has meaning. Old Testament wisdom on family relationships teaches us as parents to "impress them (spiritual truths) on your children. Talk about them when you sit at home and when you walk along the road, when you lie down and when you get up" (Deut. 6:7). The meaning that we can attach to our own life–styles should be so ingrained in us that our very actions convey a message of purposeful behavior to our children.

Because the parent is in a position to provide an atmosphere that encourages psychological growth, the personal elements he brings into the relationship with his child can impact that young person's emotional stability. A parent who has a strong sense of worth attached to his own self–concept provides a healthy model for the child to imitate. Conversely, the parent who wrestles with personal despair has difficulty providing leadership to a struggling child.

I have noted several traits in those parents who are in the best position to offer guidance to a child who experiences depression:

- Emotional stability is present. The parent's self–concept is not anchored too deeply in things such as personal achievement, material gain, status, or reputation. The parent recognizes that his value is God–given and has no strings attached.

- Showy pretenses are absent. The parent is genuine. He has accurately evaluated his own strengths and weaknesses and lives within his limitations.

- Communication with others is valued. Appropriate disclosure of thoughts, ideas, and emotions is displayed. The parent is neither too quick to tell others his troubles nor too withholding of his feelings.

- Disagreement is permitted. Recognizing that all people do not share the same views, the parent is not offended when others differ with him.

- Respect from others is earned. The parent recognizes that a leadership style that discourages input from others creates unrest among his children. Leadership that takes into account the opinions of all of the family members encourages cooperation.

- A giving spirit is displayed. A proper balance is maintained between looking out for selfish needs and willingly providing for the needs of others.

- When commitments are made, they are kept. All responsibilities that range from those of relative unimportance to those of primary importance are viewed as being significant. Action is taken on promises made.

The model displayed by the parent speaks volumes to a child or teenager who may need emotional guidance. In most cases, the child observes the parent as he develops strategies for coping with his trials. The parent whose own life is solidly grounded on principals of spiritual worth and who demonstrates a positive approach to parental responsibilities is a great resource for a struggling child.

Summary

While everyone experiences times in which they feel down, a sizeable number of children and adolescents feel chronically depressed. This disorder is growing in its prevalence, striking young people at all ages and social classes. The most common characteristics of a depressed condition include:

- A loss of interest in routine activities.

- Failure to reach potential level of capabilities.

- Lowered sense of self–worth.

- Difficulty communicating emotions.

- Common complaints of physical discomfort.

- Willingness to take risks.

- Lack of a sense of direction and purpose in life.

Depression may result from influences that are outside the direct control of a child, or from a child's tendency to react to his world. The most common contributors to childhood depression are:

- Stress factors ranging from numerous mild traumas to events and circumstances that could be life–changing in their impact.

- A personality style of sensitivity creating a proneness to depression.

- Negative responses from others that cause discouragement.

- A home atmosphere in which adults model depressed behavior.

The parent can exert control over many factors that encourage a child to feel depressed. As the leader of the household, parents should try to understand how the child views his own world. Management of depressed behavior includes:

- Identifying and controlling the effects of stress on a child to the extent possible.

- Making an effort to redirect a child's negative beliefs in himself.

- Avoiding behavior patterns that serve to perpetuate negative feelings within the child.

- Giving positive verbal rewards that the child cannot refuse.

- Increasing motivation by giving frequent rewards.

- Accepting the child's communication efforts, even negative statements.

- Demonstrating a life–style that is genuine and full of meaning.

Session 1

Study Session Objective:

To recognize the various ways depression may be displayed in your child and its effect on his behavior.

Biblical Reference: Book of Jonah

Throughout this account, Jonah struggled with depression. His depression was seen not only in his emotional despondency, but also in his disobedience. As you read the Book of Jonah, notice the wide variations in Jonah's moods and actions.

Discussion Questions:

1. What are the more obvious ways your child displays feelings of depression?

2. What are the more subtle ways your child displays feelings of depression? What does this say about his ability to communicate how he feels?

3. What role do you perceive anger to play in the development of a depressed condition? What about other emotions such as fear, guilt, or worry?

4. In what ways does our present–day society lead children into a life–style of emptiness and a feeling of spiritual despair? What elements of family life can encourage similar feelings?

5. What are some events or circumstances that seem traumatic to a child or teenager but seem relatively insignificant to adults? Why do young people interpret these things as they do?

Assignments:

1. Begin to groom a communication skill that conveys to your child that you understand him. Have at least one dialogue per day in which you focus only on the child's point of view. Paraphrase to him what he has told you, ask for clarification, or tell him you want to know more.

2. Take an active stance in approaching your child. Play a game with him or take him on an outing. Don't be discouraged if he is not outwardly appreciative of your gesture. He's only being cautious.

Session 2

Study Session Objective:
To learn to address the communication and management issues that are often contributors to childhood depression.

Biblical Reference: Isa. 43:1–7
Isaiah tells of God's undying faithfulness to His children. Despite the errors of His children, God never fails to bring them back under His care.

Discussion Questions:

1. In what ways do you send nonverbal messages to your child that may become barriers to communication?

2. What communication patterns can you identify that result in a breakdown of healthy dialogue? What is it about these exchanges that prevents meaningful conversation?

3. What evidences can you identify to show that your child responds better to rewards and reinforcement than to criticism and punishment? If there seems to be little evidence that he responds to a positive approach, what could be some of the contributing factors?

4. Why do you think so many parents are so quick to render their judgments, opinions, or constructive criticisms in response to their children's words or behaviors? Do you think most parents are unwilling to allow their children to learn lessons about life through experience? Why or why not?

Assignments:

1. Appropriately express your spiritual belief about a moral issue that arises in the next few days. Avoid "preaching" to

your child, and yet give him the feeling that he can count on you for direction and guidance. Leave room for healthy questioning of your beliefs by the child. He learns through his interactions with you.

2. Conduct an "attitude study" of your family. Give an honest appraisal of the general mood of the home. Keep doing those things that are positive. Work on eliminating the negative.

5

As the World Turns (Around Me)—

The Self-Centered Teenager

—*Case Study*—

SEVENTEEN–YEAR–OLD HANK HAD BECOME unreasonable to live with over the past few years. Always a demanding child, his expectations of others had reached the point that it was impossible to please him. In the past, Hank's parents had been pretty successful in their efforts to satisfy their son's desires. Not a wealthy family, they had made sacrifices to give him the pleasures of life they had not experienced. It seemed, though, that the more they gave to him, the more he expected.

As a young adolescent, most of Hank's requests were for things such as name–brand clothes, special privileges, or gadget items that appealed to him. But now the expectations he had of his parents were beyond those normally held by other teenagers. He didn't want just any car to drive, he wanted an expensive one with a loud stereo system in it. He wanted no curfew and no limitations on his social activities. He expected a handsome weekly allowance to accommodate his extravagant tastes. What's worse, he even wanted his mother to provide a maid service because he didn't feel it his duty to keep his room cleaned.

Hank's parents, Mr. and Mrs. Beck, realized their error in allowing him to become so self-absorbed. However, they felt helpless to change their ways with him. When they tried to say no to his requests, he threw terrible tantrums. He would follow them around the house arguing with such tenacity that they felt compelled to give in to him simply to allow for a few moments of peace. One time Hank even went as far as to swallow several pills with the threat of swallowing more if his parents did not succumb to his demands.

Mr. and Mrs. Beck knew their son needed professional guidance, but he refused help whenever it was mentioned. He would not admit to feelings of depression despite its obvious presence. He refused to consider himself as weak or vulnerable to feelings of low self-esteem. He reasoned that if others would cooperate with him, his life would be completely normal.

Defining the Self-Centered Teenager

Our current generation is seeing a tremendous influx of children, especially adolescents, who meet the criteria of self-centeredness. Part of the increase in the number of self-centered youth is due to the increasing emphasis our world places on values such as status, position, title, material gain, and public prestige. Among the many biblical references condemning self-centeredness is Philippians 2:3. Paul teaches us to avoid selfishness and empty conceit. Yet there is more emphasis on competitiveness and individual achievement today than there has been at any point in history. Our youth are growing up in a world that strongly encourages them to put themselves first and others second.

A second driving force behind the emergence of unusual self-centeredness in some of today's youth is the mistaken belief that a good parent is one who makes life easy for his child. I certainly do not advocate a system of values that puts the child in a position of hardship. However, in many family circles, a proper balance has not been achieved to encourage the child to respect all that he is as a person or all that the world has to offer him.

I will speak of the self-centered adolescent since it is typically during these years that the characteristics of this problem become clearly evident. Its roots generally extend into earlier years, but the problems of self-centeredness are usually stronger during the teenage years. The difficulty of managing this teenager lies in the years of deception that have typically occurred with the child convincingly explaining that he will conform to parental demands if only certain conditions are met.

The most common characteristics of the self–centered teenager are as follows:

Unusual emphasis on the importance of self. Pride is not necessarily a negative term, for it can denote a feeling of well–deserved satisfaction over a job adequately done. But pride can be carried to an extreme. Paul tells us how we can allow pride to be a display of our own foolishness (Rom. 1:22). The self–centered adolescent will feel a special sense of importance that leads him to feel set apart from others. This special feeling may exist even though there is limited reason for the teenager to feel that way.

For example, I know of a 16–year–old boy who took great pride in his ability to fool his piano teacher. His brilliance as a pianist allowed him to not have to practice as much as an average student would require. Therefore, he would neglect practicing the piano during the week only to do relatively well at his piano lesson. He failed to recognize that his own level of performance would be greatly enhanced by a more concerted effort.

Because the teenager views himself as being above the norms that are used to judge his peers, great humiliation is experienced when a flaw is exposed. The normal reaction of the self–centered youth is to place blame on someone else for allowing this imperfection to be exposed.

The young pianist would feel justified in blaming his piano teacher for his own poor performance on a piece of music. Rather than admit his need for more rehearsal time, the teenager could accuse the teacher of purposely assigning music that was beyond reasonable expectations or he could complain that he was distracted by an argument with his girlfriend earlier in the day. Whatever the reason for his flawed performance, the self–centered teen would find someone or some circumstance on which to place blame.

High self–esteem is deceptive. Beneath the feelings of inflated self–importance are normally hidden feelings of low self–worth. One of my mentors told me to be aware that a reason always exists for every behavior and emotion that a child or adolescent displays. Actions and feelings do not present themselves in a random fashion. He also explained to me that some youth will provide direct answers to the question, "Why is that behavior or emotion present?" Others will require more intensive searching for the answer to this question. Such is the case with the self–centered teenager.

Beneath the facade of superiority lies a strong sense of inferiority. We can uncover the self–centered adolescent's low self–image by contrasting the behaviors of this person to that of one who feels more secure in himself. The following chart gives us a comparison:

Weak Self–Esteem	Healthy Self–Esteem
Quick to criticize others	Willing to encourage others
Holds grudges against adversaries	Lets go of unnecessary anger
Unwilling to accept criticism	Considers critical remarks
Fails to admit weaknesses	Knows personal limitations
Makes strong demands of others	Considerate of others
Deceptive communication	Open communication
Dogmatic and opinionated	Secure beliefs, but open–minded
Wants to be in control	Cooperates with others
Withholds feelings	Shares feelings appropriately
Preoccupied with self	Interested in others
Unpredictable moods	Stable moods
Emphasizes materialism	Emphasizes relationships
Not satisfied by compliments	Graciously accepts compliments
Enjoys seeing others fail	Enjoys others' success
Blames others for faults	Recognizes personal limitations

The behavioral and emotional expressions of the self–centered teenager contradict the statements he may make as he boasts of feelings of positive self–esteem. A general rule of thumb that applies to self–centered adolescents is that behaviors always speak louder than words in describing the true character of a person.

Behaviors may be overly dramatized. The self-centered teenager feels a sense of panic when he detects a loss of control. This youth feels in control when he is convinced that others are accepting the deception he displays. When adults, or even other teenagers, refuse to respond to the adolescent's desire for control, a major eruption in behavior is often the result. In keeping with his deception, however, the outburst is typically more intended for manipulative purposes than as an expression of honest emotion.

—Case Study—

Over the period of several weeks, 15-year-old Warren had been engaged in a series of behaviors that were inconsistent with the guidelines his parents, Mr. and Mrs. Collins, had established for him. On two consecutive weekends, he had spent the night with a friend whose parents allowed their son and Warren to stay out an hour longer than Warren's normal curfew. Warren explained to his mother and father that there was no wrong involved since his friend's parents had sanctioned the curfew hour.

On a third weekend Warren attended a party at which alcohol was served. Mr. and Mrs. Collins were concerned about their son associating with youth who habitually drank to the point of intoxication because they realized he was susceptible to negative peer pressure. Yet, Warren argued that there was nothing wrong with his attendance at the party since he had not become drunk and had not gotten involved in serious misconduct.

On this particular weekend, Mr. Collins felt the need to impose some controls on Warren in an effort to prevent him from getting into behaviors that were more than just questionable. He told Warren that he would not be allowed to spend the night at the house of his friend. As a concession, however, Warren would be allowed to invite the friend to spend the night at the Collins' home so that closer supervision could be provided.

Dad braced himself for the predictable storm that followed. Although Warren vehemently voiced his objections to his dad's limitations, he grudgingly succumbed to his father's will when he realized that he was not going to win the fight.

Not one to give up easily, Warren approached his mother once his father had left the room. He begged her to intercede on his behalf and to attempt to change his father's mind.

"Please, Mother! Talk to Dad. Tell him to let me spend the night at Troy's house. We already have plans. We're not going to get into any trouble, I promise!"

Mom wouldn't agree to Warren's plan. "Warren, you've heard what your dad said. I'm not going to talk to him about it. I know he won't change his mind."

With that Warren began to sob loudly. "Mom, I can't tell you how much I want to go to Troy's. I need the break from home! I need to get away for a night! Please, Mom, let me go!" He continued to beg and cry with his mother.

Intent on showing unity with Warren's father, Mom again responded negatively to her son's pleas. "Son, it's no use to cry like that. You already know what my answer is. I'm not going to change my mind."

With those words Warren's tears dried immediately. His expression instantly changed to one filled with scorn. "Mom, I thought you loved me, but you don't. If you loved me, you'd see that spending the night with Troy is what I need to do. You'd want me to go because it would make me happy. But you don't love me like I thought you did. Well, I want you to know that I don't love you either."

This emotional demonstration by Warren is indicative of the kind of dramatization practiced by the self–centered adolescent. Although the teenager would have the parent believe that his emotions are truly from the heart, his actual intent is to use these expressions as a weapon with the purpose of manipulation. Over the course of time, the teenager can become quite convincing and is able to successfully deceive others.

Relationships with others are intense. The self–centered teenager is often a well–liked person. Being keenly aware of his status among his peers, he is careful to exercise great care in cultivating relationships. It is important to be included in the right social group and to be known by a wide range of acquaintances. Most self–centered adolescents are known to an abundance of other teenagers and, in many cases, are well thought of by their peers.

The relationship this teenager has with his closest friends will often differ greatly from what most people experience with him. Close friends and family members typically see a side of this person that is off limits to all others. Frequently, the intensity of the personality is especially evident in close relationships with the opposite sex.

As a result of his own need to be the most important part of a relationship, the self–centered youth is attracted to a member of the opposite sex that will soothe his need for control. Thus, a less domineering and emotionally passive friend is commonly sought.

Emotional intensity within the relationships of the self–centered teenager may be manifested in various ways including:

- Frequent squabbles over petty matters.
- Jealousy over friendships that interfere with the relationship.
- Long hours spent in conversation often resulting in little resolve.
- Preoccupation with that relationship to the exclusion of others.
- Unreasonable demands on the other individual.
- Difficulty dismissing a relationship that has run its course.

Because selected relationships are of such strength, much of the teenager's emotional health hinges on the stability between himself and those to whom he is most closely attached. Feelings of euphoria are common when relationships are strong. Deep depression is the result of difficulties in the relationship.

—Case Study—

Carol was a physically attractive 18 year old who seemed to have everything going for her. She was beautiful, capable of maintaining good grades, a school cheerleader, and a class officer for her senior class in high school. Other girls who knew Carol were frequently heard to say they wished they were as fortunate as she. Life seemed to always go the right way for her.

Despite her outward success and popularity, Carol was very depressed. She came to me as a result of her inability to sleep and her recurring thoughts about the uselessness of her life. She told me she had revealed to a friend that she was receiving personal counseling and that her friend was shocked that Carol had any personal adjustment problems. She simply seemed too perfect for such flaws.

Most of Carol's conversation centered around a broken relationship with a teenaged boy with whom she felt she was truly in love. After a two year period of time, her boyfriend had severed the relationship stating he could no longer bear the emotional rollercoaster ride she had caused him. Unable to accept rejection from others, Carol went into a deep depression that even her good friends did not fully comprehend.

Carol's preoccupation with her lost boyfriend dealt not with a desire to recapture a relationship, but with the shame she felt at not conquering him emotionally. The impact of the breakup jolted her feeling of universal control over others. She could not bear the thought that someone considered her to be undesirable.

Irresponsible behavior is commonly displayed. The self–centered teenager possesses a sense of entitlement. It is his belief that the responsibilities and expectations placed on others do not apply to him. He is the exception to the rule. He will feel insulted if asked to participate in mundane activities such as mowing the yard, taking trash to a garbage can, cleaning his bedroom, completing his homework, or washing his laundry.

This adolescent feels that rules should be broken for him. He argues that he is more mature than the average teenager and is thus capable of being treated more as an adult than a teenager. For this reason he feels he should be allowed privileges such as driving a car even though he is too young to obtain a driver's license. Dating at a very young age does not seem unreasonable to this youth. Control of a checking account or credit card will not be viewed by him as risky.

Related to the adolescent's feeling that rules should be bent for him is a belief that he is not accountable for his behavior in the same way that others are. Even when authority figures insist that the teen show cooperation, that teen will not understand the need to demonstrate evidence that he is indeed doing what he said he would. His disdain for accountability is related to his fear of losing control of his desired life–style. To be accountable to others would call for increased responsibility.

—Case Study—

There were many times that Mr. and Mrs. Walker felt they had made a mistake in buying their teenaged son, Ricky, a car. They had hoped Ricky would consider the auto as a prize possession and care for it. They had reasoned that the responsibility of his own vehicle would encourage him to learn to manage his money and even his time more appropriately. They were disappointed when time proved them to be wrong.

Within the first year of receiving the car, Ricky accumulated two traffic tickets and his car gained a couple of unsightly dents. His tendency to drive like a race–car driver had worn on the engine, causing various mechanical failures. Ricky vowed to fix these minor problems, but never fulfilled his promises.

Prior to having his own car, Ricky had complained that he was frequently late coming home or arriving at other destinations because he was at the whim of his friends' unpredictable schedules. Yet, having his own transportation had no effect on his own punctuality and, in fact, created even more problems in that area of concern.

When his parents talked with him about the management of his car, Ricky was quick to become defensive. He was offended by his parents' suggestion that he limit his driving to certain times or circumstances. He proclaimed that it was none of their business how he drove the car as long as he got to his destination in one piece. He refused to give an account for where he went or what he did. But he did become angry when his parents promised to cut his car allowance if some cooperation on his part was not displayed.

Emotions are often exaggerated. It is normal for teenagers to have mood swings that are fairly wide. Yet, the emotions of the self–centered adolescent vary even greater than is typical for his age level. When the teenager experiences a success (according to his criteria), the feeling of euphoria is described as unbelievably strong. Conversely, should disappointment be encountered, the low feeling can only be portrayed by the adolescent as depression.

Ricky's irresponsible actions are typical of a pattern shown by many self–absorbed adolescents. Not only did Ricky show a tendency toward irresponsible behavior, but he also was inappropriate in his display of emotions. His dramatic emotional expressions were aimed at manipulating others and were not an honest expression of his feelings.

Depression is a very common emotion for the self–centered teenager. Because this young person is preoccupied with how others perceive him, any sign of personal failure creates a strong sense of humiliation. Often, these private feelings of inadequacy are concealed as the adolescent hides behind masks such as indifference, outrage, or excessive pride. True emotional expression is infrequently disclosed to others. It is often necessary to look beneath the surface of the adolescent's behavior to discover the meaning attached to it.

Examples of the exaggerated emotions this teenager may display are wide ranging:

- A 14 year old feels very rugged and proud when he scores a touchdown even though he is only playing a sandlot game with other relatively nonathletic teens. His immense pride stems from the fact that several girls witnessed his feat. He assumes that they were inspired by his accomplishment.

- An attractive girl fishes for compliments from others after getting her hair cut and styled. Though many of the flattering comments were made only because they were solicited, the girl swells internally with a keen awareness of her own beauty.

- When passed over by the drama coach for a key part in a play, a youth is indignant at the adult's uncommon lack of judgment. Privately, he shows his feelings of rage to an astonished friend. He threatens to drop out of the drama cast because he cannot bear to associate with a drama coach who is incompetent and unable to spot obvious talent.

- Feeling above the rules of the classroom, a student in his junior English class feels no guilt after cheating on a major exam. He rationalizes by saying, "I made an 'A,' didn't I? The most important thing is to be able to cheat without getting caught."
- A 17–year–old boy not only feels hurt by the breakup with his girlfriend, he is crushed. It provides him no consolation for others to point out that teenage relationships dissolve daily.

At the root of his depressed mood is a disbelief that his girl-friend would even consider splitting up with him. He cannot conceive of her attaching herself to another boy who could be better for her than he was.

Through a self–centered style of perceiving the world, there develops a tunnel vision view of life. Events are not interpreted in light of their impact on others, but solely upon their impact on the teenager. There is little objectivity in this adolescent, dooming him to learn lessons about life through repeated mistakes. Frequently this lack of objectivity leads to an inappropriate emotional response from the teen.

Factors Influencing the Self–Centered Teenager's Behavior

Good intentions may go awry. It is common for parents to desire for their child a life–style that surpasses that of their own youth. We have all heard others say, "I want to give my child the things I could not have when I was young." It is assumed that our children will appreciate our overtures toward them and will greatly value the pleasures provided them. Yet, too often good intentions fail, and the result is an unappreciative teenager who only wants more and more. The admonition to "discipline your son, for in that there is hope" (Prov. 19:18) may be neglected on the chance that the child will change his behavior of his own volition.

A parental mistake is made when the parent fails to use the word "no" at appropriate times during the child's early years. I certainly am not advocating that parents be stingy with their children. I do suggest, however, that a healthy balance be maintained in which the child is given responsibilities along with rewards and privileges.

—Case Study—

I first got to know Dean when he was seven years old and in the second grade. He was a boy virtually everyone liked. He was well–mannered and seldom violated rules willfully. His friends and playmates got along well with him. At home he created few discipline problems for his parents.

As an only child, Dean had the full attention of his parents. In fact, the household schedule revolved around the boy's wants and desires. Suppertime came when Dean was finished playing outside. Bedtime was set according to Dean's TV viewing schedule. Weekend activities centered around the things he was interested in.

While Dean was young, the parents' way of managing their son seemed to be effective. He seemed to appreciate the conciliatory manner in which his parents treated him. The emergence of adolescence, however, saw their quiet, undemanding child become increasingly difficult to discipline.

During the junior high school years, Dean developed the habit of going to bed very late, making it difficult for his parents to arouse him in the mornings before school. Once home from school, he would frequently sleep, neglecting his homework and household chores. As he got older, he eventually quit school, saying he felt he could make a better life for himself by working. His parents reasoned that school was not for everyone and perhaps Dean would be better off working at a job. At least he would have to be responsible to a boss or employer. Perhaps it would be a good experience for him.

Dean's plan failed to work as he had hoped. He was unable to keep a job because of his lack of punctuality and general irresponsibility. Without steady work, he could not move out of his parents' home. He continued to rely on his mom and dad to support his life–style. In fact, he expected his parents to sustain him. At age 19, Dean had developed no more concern for his own responsibilities than he had as a boy.

Dean's parents recognized their error with their son. Although their intent during his early years had been to make life comfortable for him, they had made his life *too* comfortable. Assuming that Dean would value the freedoms they gave him, he learned to take them for granted. When they tried to teach him the need to look beyond his present wishes and desires, he refused to listen to their counsel. The good idea of providing their son with an easy life–style collapsed as Dean failed to experience any discomforts that could have contributed to his personal growth.

Boundaries may be too broad or too narrow. One of the facts about human nature is that people do not respond well to authority figures that are either too constrictive or too vague. This truth seems to be especially applicable to children. I frequently hear children and teenagers complain of having to follow too many rules. I have seen the often negative effects of a household in which the child feels choked by the multiplicity of regulations he is expected to follow. In a surprisingly similar way, there are also harmful effects on the child who has few guidelines to follow.

Adolescents who have been raised in a loosely structured home often have at least one thing in common with those who come from a more restrictive home environment. That common ground is a tendency to become too keenly occupied with oneself. The expression of that self–centeredness may differ, but the desire to put self before all other things is present in both.

Ways in which the adolescent from a very restrictive home environment may show his self–centered nature include:

- Attempting to force his needs to be recognized by others through active rebellion.

- Passive refusal to comply with even the simplest of demands.

- Withdrawal from others to protect himself from being emotionally hurt.

- Adopting a life–style that is "different" as a means of expressing his individuality.

- Leaving home and maintaining little contact with family members.

- Developing a cynical attitude of suspicion toward anyone who differs from himself.

- Forcing outrageous demands and expectations upon others.

Ways in which the adolescent from a very loosely structured home environment may show his self–centered nature include:

- Displaying no concern for others' schedules or time constraints.

- Failure to spend money wisely; poor money management.

- Making promises and not living up to them.

- Establishing no sense of direction or purpose to life.

- Difficulty making decisions and sticking with them.

- Inability to say no to any activity that brings momentary joy.

- Easily influenced by others who promise quick gratification.

Although each set of behavioral characteristics differs in its outward display, the message beneath each remains the same: "I come before anything or anyone else." Thus, it is conceivable that teenagers from constricted home environments and those from more loosely structured homes will exhibit similar behaviors. Those from restrictive homes act self–centered out of a sense of rebellion due to years of not being allowed to express internal feelings. Teens from homes with little or no structure tend to act self–centered as a result of a lack of guidance that teaches the need to consider the needs of others.

The commonality for each group of adolescents is that neither has been provided with appropriate behavioral boundaries that lead to a proper awareness of the needs of others. While children have the capacity to care for others, that characteristic needs to be fostered through the provision of well–balanced parental guidance. Too much or too little direction from the parent can result in a preoccupation with oneself on the part of the adolescent.

Peer pressure encourages self–centeredness. The phenomenon of peer pressure and its influence on the teenager is complex. Even teenagers themselves recognize the dangers involved in allowing others to have too great an influence on the decisions they make. Yet, human beings are gregarious. We all like to be with others. It is important to feel as if we fit in.

The response of the adolescent to peer pressure is variable. Some teens are fully aware of their personal strengths and weak- nesses and know where to draw the line when it comes to coercion at the hand of other teenagers. There are many other teenagers, however, who fail to recognize their own limitations and fall prey to negative influences. These teenagers who become susceptible to developing a life–style of self–centeredness focus primarily on the self and little on others.

Several personal characteristics are often present in adoles- cents who are more prone to succumbing to the negative influences of others:

- A strong desire to feel important which arises from a low self–esteem.

- A willingness to compromise personal values in order to gain acceptance from others.

- An unwillingness to assert himself in the presence of others who are viewed as important figures.

- Fear of feeling rejected by others.

- A need for attention from peers because others don't seem to understand him.

- Determines right and wrong on the basis of a popular vote.

Once a teenager is caught in the vicious cycle of trying to keep up with the demands of his peer group, he can become absorbed in a pattern of thought that encourages him to exclude the needs of others. Even those adolescents who are well aware of the negative influence other teenagers can have on them find themselves fighting to avoid the lure toward self–centeredness.

—Case Study—

Fourteen–year–old Roland was experiencing a tremendous internal struggle. He had been raised in a home which emphasized high moral values. His parents stressed to him, both in word and action, the importance of being sensitive to the needs of others. Roland had been successful in developing commendable social skills. But, he admitted that the coercion he received from others to give in to a different form of behavior was becoming unbearably strong.

"Last weekend I went to a party at a friend's house and for the first time I was afraid I would give in to my friends," Roland began his story.

"Your friends were making it hard for you to turn them down," I responded to him. I knew Roland wanted to say much more.

"I was really mad at this guy named Peter. He's supposed to be one of my best friends. But, he had tasted some Coke that had gin in it and wanted me to drink some, too. He tried to convince me that it would taste good." Roland's voice sounded uncertain.

"And you weren't too sure how to react to him." I continued to listen.

"Well, I knew I shouldn't drink it because it's not healthy and my parents have told me why I shouldn't drink alcohol. But I kinda wanted to just try it out." Roland developed a look of guilt over his face as he admitted to his desire.

"No doubt there were a lot of different thoughts running through your mind," I responded.

"Yeah, I didn't want my parents to find out that I had tasted alcohol, but I didn't want my friends to think I was a prude. I was really mad at Peter for trying to make me choose. He kept on bugging me about trying the drink so I finally did. I didn't like it, but I pretended I did. I was so confused I didn't know what to do."

Many adolescents have had experiences similar to Roland's. Unprepared for the tremendous pressure thrust on them, they are surprised at themselves after having succumbed to the demands of others. I have counseled many youth who have expressed shame and guilt following a long pattern of self–centeredness that was largely encouraged by demanding peers.

Parents struggle over the loss of control of their teenaged child. The respect the teenager had for adults as a youngster often seems to disappear for several years. In its place is an attitude that forces individual needs to come first and the needs of others to be placed on a back burner.

There exists a cycle of influence from others that is common to most children and adolescents. From birth through the age of about 10–12 the most important source of influence comes from the family. Family ties represent the most desirable relationships to the young child. But as the child enters early adolescence, the peer group replaces the family as the most important source of behavioral control. It is not until early adulthood, when the young adult becomes involved in establishing a family of his own, that the individual moves away from the peer group and relies once again on the family as the most important source of influence in his life.

Perhaps one of the most frustrating aspects of parenting a teenager is the sense of lost control over that young person due to the pressures of the peer group. The parent's feeling of desperation can lead to a pattern of conflict with the child that seems to be endless. Teenagers are quick to recognize the tension they have created and will actually take advantage of an opportunity to assert their control. Signs that tell the adolescent that his parent is losing the battle of control to the peer group include:

- The parent's failure to view the reality, and even the necessity, of the peer group's influence on the teen.

- A parent's tendency to become very restrictive in hopes of silencing the teenager's rebellion.

- Relinquishing all efforts to place constraints on the teenager.

- An increase in critical remarks, coupled with a decrease in supportive statements.

Given the inevitable nature of peer pressure on most adolescents, the parents who fail to adjust parental styles to the developmental stage of the teenager are subject to repeated frustration. The parent is not without options in confronting the problem of peer group pressure on the adolescent. The task of the parent must shift during these years to a role that continues to actively manage the family while dealing with the reality of the pressures that encourage the adolescent to put himself before all others.

Society's assault on the teenager can be harmful. Closely akin to peer group pressures are the strains the teenager feels from society. The increased visibility of self–centered teenagers in today's world represents a reflection of a culture that urges individuals to put self first and others last. In some instances, the pressures put upon the teens are blatant while other invitations to give in to desire are masked in a more subtle fashion. I see evidence of society's pressure on the adolescent as coming from three sources.

1. **Media Influence**. The development of mass communication opportunities has had a tremendous impact on the development of today's society and cultures. Statistics show that a frightening percentage of children and adolescents (as well as adults) spend more time under the influence of the media than with any combined group of people. An adventuresome

existence, or a life—style in which endings are always happy, or where fantasies are realized, emotions graphically expressed, or aggressions released has tremendously strong appeal to children and youth.

Many impressionable youth are slowly seduced into developing a point of view that overemphasizes self—gratification. Too many teenagers fail to recognize the strong grip the media has on them. In their way of thinking, their adopted philosophy of life cannot be all wrong since it is so widespread.

2. **Change in family structure.** In the past, the typical family was composed of a mother, father, and their children. The father worked in an occupation outside the home while the mother worked at home and took control of domestic matters. Today, such a "typical" family does not exist. There are many common family constellations including:

- The "traditional" family with mother, father, and their children.

- The blended family of husband, wife, and any combination of his children, her children, and their children.

- The single parent family with mother and her children.

- The single parent family with father and his children.

- The "common law" family with an unmarried man and woman and any combination of his and her children.

- The unwed teenaged mother, her children, and the maternal grandparent(s).

There are even more family patterns in our society than those listed above, but they are less common. The fact facing the teenager today is that there is a lack of security attached to today's family. That loss of certainty within family relations often is translated by the adolescent as a signal to protect self first since the guarantee of assistance from others is not always strong.

3. **Shift in ethical and moral standards.** With society's shift from an orientation that put others in equality to self to a

stance in which self is preeminent has come a change in our definition of right and wrong. That shift in moral and ethical judgment has been so subtle that many have not noticed the change it has rendered in our public life. Many forms of conduct that were once considered morally wrong were initially resisted, then tolerated, and finally accepted. Witness the following moral and ethical changes that have taken place over the last few decades:

- Once reserved for marriage, sexual activity and promiscuity among youth is now common.

- Intoxication by alcohol or other substances is representative of the macho style of life. Abstainers are considered to be weaklings.

- Regard for law and order is held in disregard even among the most public members of society.

- Guilt over wrongdoing is easily replaced by the security that many others have committed the same act.

- Homosexuality is now seen as an alternative life–style rather than one that is unnatural.

- Abortion offers a choice to end a "mistake" before it creates a need to become responsible.

With each of these factors being imposed on today's children and adolescents there is little wonder that our young people are more easily giving in to the lure to place selfish needs before the needs of others. The constant encouragement to put self before all else encourages compromise. The high frequency of public compliance to society's pressure gives the teenager a false assurance that his own self–centered behavior is right.

Adolescence itself demands attention. Have you ever stopped to consider all the major changes that occur during the adolescent years? An abbreviated list of the changes nature forces on the teenager includes the following:

- Learning to get along socially with the opposite sex.

- Understanding and properly channeling previously unknown sexual impulses.

- Responding to a greater degree of freedom and independence.

- Making sense out of spiritual matters.

- Acquiring complex skills such as driving a car or operating machinery.

- Deciding on preliminary career choices.

- Communicating emotions and feelings in an understandable manner.

- Learning to think independently from what Mom and Dad think.

- Earning and spending money in a responsible fashion.

Now that's quite a list! The demands life places on adolescents are greater during those few years than at any other time in life. With so many tasks to achieve and so little knowledge of how to accomplish them, it is little wonder adolescence has such a negative reputation. In many ways the teen years force self–centeredness because of their great demands.

One college–aged young man told me with a sense of exasperation, "I'm glad I won't be a teenager much longer. I'm tired!" Unfortunately, he was doomed to the realization that adulthood brings its own unique set of circumstances, but he deserved to feel at least momentary relief knowing that the adolescent years were almost over.

Managing the Self–Centered Teenager

Changing the self–centered teenager into one who more willingly views the world from the point of view of others is no easy task. Perhaps the most difficult aspect of redirecting a self–centered adolescent lies in the fact that he is likely to be determined to learn lessons about life the hard way. Witnessing the inevitable mistakes this adolescent must make in order to eventually adjust to a world in which he is not the center of attention is difficult for most parents. And yet such an experience is often necessary. The wisdom of Proverbs informs the parent that "a child left to itself disgraces his mother," but provides reassurance that when that child is given correction "he will give you peace" and will also "bring delight to your soul" (Prov. 29:15, 17).

The parent's role in helping to manage self–centeredness includes the need to let the teenager conclude for himself that it is in his own best interest to learn to coexist with others in a healthy manner. The following guidelines give direction in that regard.

Establish boundaries and stick with them. Most self–centered teenagers seem to believe that rules were made for others and not for themselves. Their strong sense of self–importance makes them feel above the guidelines that other adolescents must comply with. As noted earlier, this teen will experience humiliation when asked to succumb to the norms that are expected of his age group. He has come to believe that adults, especially parents, who attempt to impose restrictions on him are simply unaware of his unusual need for independence.

I like to view behavior management of children and adolescents in terms of the child's needs. Doing so allows the parents to maintain a greater sense of objectivity with their child. With this point in mind, the parent can be easily convinced that it is in the teenager's best interest that he learn to consider others' needs as well as his own. Thus, even though momentary pleasure may be experienced by a child who has been allowed to have his way, his long–term interests will be better served by hearing the word now spoken to him.

—Case Study—

Fifteen–year–old Alfred had become more difficult to manage over the period of two to three years. His parents, Mr. and Mrs. Hutchins, explained their son had developed an attitude that put his own needs before all others. They recognized that their approach of providing for all of Alfred's needs and desires had not met with the intended result. Rather than learning to appreciate all he had, Alfred took all things for granted. Mr. Hutchins defended himself as he examined the behavior pattern of his son, "It didn't really matter to me what Alfred did as long as it was safe and he was enjoying himself."

Having agreed that it was in Alfred's best interest to learn to accept limits, the Hutchinses decided to implement a new plan of action. They knew Alfred had intentions to fish all day on the upcoming Saturday. Yet, there were several chores in the yard that needed attention as well. It was agreed that prior to going fishing, Alfred would be required to complete some yard work. The Hutchinses were further instructed that Alfred would probably argue loudly at the demands placed on him, but they were to refrain from engaging in a conflict with him. The boundary was to be firmly adhered to.

Alfred's reaction to his parents' arrangement was predictable. He argued with his parents when told of the expectations they had of him. He complained that it was unfair for them to compel him to do yard work on his weekend off from school. He forcefully stated that he would not comply with their request. His ranting and raving went on for most of Friday evening and on into the next day.

Having been forewarned about Alfred's probable negative reaction, the Hutchinses were able to withstand the seemingly endless barrage of complaints and threats from their son. Eventually, Alfred gave in to the reality of his assigned responsibility and completed the yard work he was required to do before going fishing. He grumbled throughout the completion of his tasks, but managed to do all that was expected of him.

Over the course of time, the Hutchinses implemented other guidelines that had not previously been a part of their discipline of Alfred. Realizing that Alfred needed behavioral guidance from them in order to develop a greater respect for the needs of others, they were able to tolerate the frequent complaints that came from their son. Rather than engage in their old habit of negotiating with him (which usually resulted in "success" for Alfred), they maintained control of their emotions and became more effective in their positive influence over their son.

The behavior pattern of the self–centered child is often quite similar to that of the oppositional child. In order to assert his sense of self–importance, he often engages others in power struggles. The goal of these struggles is to coerce the parent to give way to the teenager's self–centered desires.

As with the oppositional child, it is not enough to make guidelines and then stick with them. Emotional control must also be maintained. In so doing, the adult can successfully allow the teenager to focus on the responsibility he has for his actions. To lose emotional control encourages the adolescent to relinquish responsibility for his own behavior to the adult since the adult is obviously heavily invested in the problem at hand.

Avoid communication that causes humiliation. The way parents communicate with children has a great deal to do with the eventual cooperation shown by the young person. The manner in which the adult talks to the self–centered teenager will strongly influence the reaction he displays. Because this adolescent is keenly aware of his status among others, he is quite sensitive to comments that have the intent or effect of making him appear to be inadequate. While virtually all children respond poorly to negativism, the self–centered one is most likely to become hostile when adults use tactics causing feelings of humiliation. The following are among the more common communication approaches to be avoided:

- Sarcasm that allows others to laugh in a snide way about the teenager's faults.

- Bringing up the past as evidence of the adolescent's negative points.

- Threats that cause the teen to feel challenged to a "duel."

- The use of colorful adjectives to describe the teenager's personality.

- Lectures aimed at developing logic within the youth.

- Predictions about what is likely to happen in the event the teen makes a poor choice.

- Accusations which show little faith in the adolescent.

—Case Study—

Fourteen–year–old Reba simply could not understand why her mother disapproved of her friendship with a classmate at school named Jamie. She knew Jamie had experienced some troubles getting along with select teachers. Yet, Reba tended to focus upon the good qualities possessed by her friend.

Reba's mother had an appreciation for the girl's emphasis on Jamie's positive points, but was too keenly aware of her daughter's tendency to be wrongly influenced by her peers. Jamie's track record for behavior problems marked her as one whom Reba should not become too closely associated with.

Reba became particularly miffed at her mother one weekend when Mom refused to allow Reba to spend the night at Jamie's house. She knew Jamie had limited supervision at home and was allowed by her mother to stay out until she felt ready to come home. Reba's lack of judgment and maturity made her a high risk for association in undesirable behavior.

"But Mom," pleaded Reba, "Why can't I stay with Jamie? We're not going to get into trouble. I promise!"

"No, Reba. You always feed into Jamie's negative behavior. I can't trust you to tell Jamie you won't go along with her actions." With those words Reba became defensive. Her good judgment had just been called into question.

"How do you know what I'll do? I just might be a positive influence on her. You always assume I'm going to get into trouble."

"You don't have the best track record, Reba. I wouldn't bet against you breaking every rule you could, or at least bending them strongly. It seems that every time Jamie has been in trouble recently, you're not far behind. I can't count on you being a positive influence on her. You girls are like two peas in a pod. You simply can't be trusted."

Reba was indignant following these comments from her mother. Rather than passively accept her mother's opinion as accurate, she continued her barrage of argumentative comments. And Mother verbally fought back. Reba's belief that her viewpoint was correct compelled her to speak her mind. Mother's equally strong feeling that Reba needed to be taught a lesson about the negative impact of the relationship she had with her chosen companion motivated her continued arguments.

The result of the conversation was that neither Reba nor her mother had altered their opinion regarding Reba's need to spend the night with her friend. Reba was not allowed to follow through with her plans so, in a sense, Mother had won the battle.

Yet, mother's mistake of causing humiliation to Reba by openly questioning her judgment assured the continuation of a war.

Mother could have more effectively managed this situation by telling Reba she could not stay overnight with her friend and then avoiding further harmful comment. Reba's predictable reaction of disagreement could have been met with a firm refusal to engage in nonproductive verbal banter. There can be little doubt that Reba was aware of her mother's thoughts and feelings about Reba's association with Jamie. To engage in a dialogue marked by negative communication decreased Mother's effectiveness as a positive influence in her daughter's life. Refraining from the use of accusations, name–calling, and predictions would have prevented much of Reba's subsequent disdain for her mother.

Because of the tendency of the self–centered teenager to exercise poor judgment regarding social matters, the duty of the parent is to provide limits that prevent the occurrence of monumental errors. The parent can expect resistance from the teen and should not be personally offended by the adolescent's disagreement. In order to avoid power struggles and the subsequent loss of emotional control that often follows, negative dialogue should be avoided.

Teach behaviors that demonstrate responsibility. Many teenagers engage in a long pattern of self–serving behaviors because they have never been taught how to demonstrate other behaviors that are aimed at anything other than personal satisfaction. I have counseled a college–aged girl who shared with me the dissatisfaction she felt about herself. As she grew to understand her own needs, she realized that she was weak in her ability to perform simple acts of kindness or consideration to others. This skill had never been groomed in her as a child. She had been raised having virtually all her needs and desires immediately met. She had not been taught responsibility and was chronically guilty of violating the needs of others. It was only as she began to live a life–style that included activities that were not solely self–serving that she felt relieved from her personal discontent.

Many parents of a self–centered teenager quietly admit that they have failed to teach their child the importance of giving to others as a part of the development of a well–rounded personality. It is surprising how many teenagers engage in very few tasks that offer service to someone else. I have heard many parents state that somehow their child has breezed through the adolescent years with few, if any, regularly assigned jobs or chores that contribute to the general welfare of the family. Continually engaging in gratifying his own needs and nobody else's promotes self–centeredness.

I do not advocate a society in which teenagers are taught the value of personal responsibility by continuous hard labor. Nonetheless, I do believe that a balance should be maintained in which the teenager learns to care not only for his own needs, but for others' needs as well.

The parent must direct the youth toward activities that contribute to the good of the whole family. Insisting that household chores be done is not likely to be met with applause by the teenager. The parent can expect a fair amount of grumbling and complaining. Yet he must not relinquish the plan requiring the teen to be responsible to others.

It is not realistic to expect a teenager to receive immediate enjoyment from completing responsibilities that are forced upon him by his parents. Few teenagers admittedly enjoy washing dishes, trimming hedges, vacuuming the house, or working in flower beds. It is acceptable, then, to provide the adolescent with an artificial reason (or motivation) for completing his assigned chores. These motivational reasons may include:

- The privilege of participating in a more desirable activity such as attending a concert or ball game.
- Receiving money resulting from a job well done.
- Verbal praise from a satisfied parent.
- An unannounced reward following the completion of a task.
- Increased parental flexibility regarding decisions directly affecting the adolescent.

Many parents have difficulty with the thought of having to reward their teenagers for completing tasks they ought to be willing to do on their own. However, since the routine completion of responsibilities is not in the self–centered adolescent's normal repertoire of behaviors, it is necessary to provide concrete motivation to the youth. Time must be allowed for the youth to decide that it was in his own best interest to develop behaviors that require him to give of himself to others.

—Case Study—

Ernie, a man in his early twenties, bought his first house in a modest neighborhood. Many of his neighbors were elderly adults. As time passed, Ernie developed a close bond with a retired couple, Mr. and Mrs. Springer, who lived across the street from him. Ernie recognized that this couple had physical limitations making it difficult for them to carry out what previously had been simple chores.

Ernie took upon himself the responsibility to help his elderly friends in a number of small ways. When a faucet washer needed to be replaced, Ernie readily assisted. He carried heavy objects that the Springers were unable to move. He even did little things such as climb a ladder to change the light bulb from the front porch light.

Ernie's older brother noticed these acts of kindness and commented to his brother, "I remember just a few short years ago that Mom and Dad had to practically beat you to get you to do any small task for them and yet now you do it willingly for the Springers. Why?"

"Because they need the help, and I'm glad to provide it," Ernie stated in a matter-of-fact way.

"But as a teenager you didn't want to take on any job unless you were paid or got something in return."

"Whatever method Mom and Dad used to get me to do a chore I'm glad they did. Had I not been required to do them, I would be helpless to be of assistance to anyone. I would even be unable to take care of the small jobs I need to do around my own house. I never thought I'd say it, but I'm glad I was taught to be responsible."

In Ernie's case, it was not until he reached adulthood that behaviors of responsibility to others became self-sustaining. As a teenager, he carried out chores because of artificial motivational incentives. Time and experience, however, taught him that responsible action toward others carries its own reward, such as internal satisfaction and the feeling of being useful to others.

Though the benefits of managing responsibilities imposed on him by others are not always readily apparent to the teen, time will allow the adolescent to recognize the satisfaction that comes from giving to others. During these teenage years, patience must be extended to the teenager while he is in the process of gaining valuable experience in life.

Eliminate family factors contributing to self–centeredness. One of the most frustrating experiences of parenthood is the feeling of helplessness that accompanies the loss of control over the temptations that confront today's adolescents. More than one parent has told me that if it were within his power such things as rock music, designer clothes, R–rated movies, expensive cars, and social clubs would all be eliminated. To do so would eliminate many of the societal forces that dominate the world of the teenager. Unfortunately, it is not possible to rid the world of its emphasis on materialism and social status. The teenager will have to learn to live in a world that is filled with vice.

Despite such a negative view, the parent is not powerless in his efforts to exert a positive influence over his own inward–prone teenager. The general atmosphere of the home teaches the adolescent many things about what is important in life. Consider the atmosphere of the household in which several of the following circumstances are present:

- Excessive attention is given to appearance, including home furnishings, clothing, type of car driven, etc.

- Conversations among family members are empty or almost nonexistent.

- Schedules are designed to meet outside social needs before family relationships.

- Family members spend much of their spare time away from one another, pursuing individual interests.

- Decisions are made without consulting one another.

- Parents and teenagers seldom engage in the same social activities.

- Parental love is demonstrated by giving gifts.

- Family problems are often unresolved because no one will listen to the others' points of view.

- Parents complain that they are too tired to engage in activities with the children.

- Angry emotions linger beyond their usefulness.

- Pride prevents the admission of mistakes.

In such a household, emphasis is placed on the parent's desire to gratify his own needs and desire. The need of the parent to provide leadership in the form of a role model and active participant in the teenager's life is unfulfilled. The atmosphere in this home is one that lends itself to the teenager becoming overly concerned about his own needs, wishes, and desires to the exclusion of other individuals. The probability, then, that the adolescent will engage in a self–centered life–style has been increased.

In contrast, consider the atmosphere of the household in which many of the following circumstances are present:

- Material needs are provided to family members but not in an excessive manner.

- Conversational topics range from simple matters to those that are more complex.

- Spare time is designed to include activities involving all members of the family.

- Individual needs are considered in making family decisions.

- Parents show a concern for the interests of the teenager.

- Parental love is shown through providing both disciplinary control and positive approval.

- Communication among family members is highlighted by a willingness to listen to the thoughts and feelings of one another.

- Family cohesion is given a high priority by parents.

- A balance is maintained in providing for the needs of all family members.

- Emotional disruptions are dealt with openly and without unnecessary emphasis.

- Reality teaches that all family members make mistakes.

A household in which the atmosphere encourages family members to look beyond their own needs and to consider the importance of involvement with one another decreases the likelihood of self-indulgence. Because the family in many ways represents a microcosm of society, the adolescent can take the attitudes taught within the family into his own world beyond the boundaries of his home.

The Apostle Paul beautifully describes the qualities of Christ (Phil. 2:5-8) which can serve as a model for parental humility. Our Lord was not consumed with His own wishes and desires; He refrained from the lust for power and status, was responsive to the needs of others, and extended Himself in an ultimate sense to all of mankind. Paul further encourages each of us to exercise humility (Phil. 2:12-15) as a way of exercising our influence on others, which certainly includes our children.

Although all members of a family are equal in their value as people, it is necessary that parents take the role of leadership because of their more advanced experiences in life. A passive role in leading the family or a leadership style that emphasizes self over others may result in a teenager who is more likely to place priority on gratifying his own needs to the exclusion of others. The mistakes that inevitably evolve from a home environment short on healthy modeling foster adolescent self-centeredness.

Summary

Self–centeredness has become characteristic of a growing number of young people in our society and is especially evident during the adolescent years. Although adolescence itself requires the individual to focus much attention on personal needs, our culture has evolved to the point that increasing emphasis is placed on putting self–gratification before other relationship needs. Parenting styles encouraging teenagers to be self–oriented have followed the course of society. Characteristics common to the self–centered teenager include:

- An exaggerated emphasis on the importance of self.

- Deceptive displays of feelings of high self–esteem.

- Behavior patterns which are overly dramatized to keep others focused on satisfying the teen's needs.

- Intense interpersonal relationships with others.

- A tendency toward irresponsible behavior.

- Exaggerated emotional expressions.

The combination of factors affecting the development of self–centered adolescent behavior includes influences both from within the home and from the environment of the teenager's world. The most common influential factors include:

- A parent's intentions of providing the "good life" to his children that minimizes the teenager's need for limitations.

- A home environment that provides either too much restriction or too much freedom.

- Peer pressure persuading the youth to conform to a common life–style.

- Society's pressure on teenagers to gratify wants and desires at the expense of others.

- The natural need of the adolescent to prepare himself for the demands of life as an adult.

The management of the self–centered teenager is made more difficult because the adolescent is often determined to learn lessons about life through the accumulation of mistakes. While the natural lessons learned through experiencing life's failures are often needed, parents can provide direction that can allow the teenager to bypass some of life's more painful truths.

- Behavioral guidelines should be established and consistently maintained.

- Communication that acknowledges the teenager's need for respect from others opens him to parental guidance.

- Responsible behavior should be taught to replace self–centered behavior.

- A family environment that provides a model of considering needs beyond those that are self–centered encourages well–rounded social behavior.

Session 1

Study Session Objective:

To understand the emergence of self-centeredness in many of today's youth.

Biblical Reference: Gen. 37:1–36; 45:1–28

The story of Joseph tells of the effects of self-centeredness in Joseph's life. Study the relationship between Joseph and his father, Jacob, to further understand the development of self-centeredness. Read Genesis 45:1–28 to show how the experiences of life brought Joseph to a position of responsibility and eventual reconciliation with his family.

Discussion Questions:

1. In what ways can a teenager be harmed by living "the good life" in which there is little to be concerned about? Does this mean parents should avoid providing good things for their children?

2. Conversely, how can a family life–style of austerity or physical need contribute to youthful self-centeredness?

3. In what ways can a teenager who seems to have things his way most of the time fall into the trap of depression and disillusionment? Do you think a self–centered teenager can fully appreciate himself as a spiritual being? Why?

4. How closely related do you believe self–centered behavior is to other sources of emotional imbalance, such as an oppositional attitude, fearfulness, sensitivity, or worry?

5. What is it about negative peer pressure that causes a teenager to succumb to temptation rather than join with others who have more positive influences?

Assignments:

1. Tell your family you will all go on a "TV diet" for one week. For that week the TV should be on for no more than five hours total viewing time. At the end of the week, discuss with the family the effects of your experiment.

2. Select two nonessential material items that you normally buy for your teenager. Give financial responsibility for these two things to your child. As time passes, increase the financial responsibility placed on your child's shoulders.

Session 2

Study Session Objective:
To move toward a behavior management style that discourages the teenager from a self–centered life–style.

Biblical Reference: Phil. 2: 5–8, 12–15
Contrast the described humility of Christ to self–centeredness. Paul offers the qualities of humility as guidelines for our lives. Model these qualities as a way of directing your child.

Discussion Questions:

1. How far should a parent go in his attempt to shield his child from the negative elements of society?

2. Do you believe it is inevitable that today's youth will be disproportionately self–centered? How much influence does the family have over this social dilemma? How much influence does the church have over teenage self–centeredness? How can these two institutions work together toward the teenager's best interest?

3. What elements are present in the atmosphere of most households that contribute to the self–centeredness of teenagers?

4. How often are most teenagers called upon to give of themselves to others in the form of work or service? How has our society encouraged teens to move away from giving of themselves to others? Has the family been too passive in encouraging adolescents to be altruistic?

5. What are some of the ways a teenager will disguise his need for adult guidance? What behaviors suggest that teens want more adult supervision and guidance?

Assignments:

1. Practice the use of the word *no* when your teenager makes unnecessary or unrealistic demands on you. Make a list of the ways your teenager attempts to convince you to change your mind. Continue in your resolve to teach your young person the value of this important word.

2. On the next occasion that you would normally offer gifts to your child, replace one material gift with a promise to perform a service for him. Look for other opportunities to teach the joy of giving of yourself to others.

6

Who, Me?
I Didn't Do It!—

The Deceitful Child

—*Case Study*—

MITCHELL WAS AN 11–YEAR–OLD BOY WHOSE habits of lying and dishonesty had been growing progressively worse over the past few months. It seemed that whenever there was a suspicion of wrongdoing, all the evidence pointed toward Mitchell. At times his parents were able to catch him in the act of lying or stealing. On other occasions, however, he was merely a suspect. Circumstantial evidence suggested his guilt, but he refused to cooperate in his parents' efforts to determine his actual involvement in the situations in question.

Mitchell's lying had become so convincing that his parents were concerned about his ability to distinguish right from wrong. In their talks with one another, Mother and Dad questioned their son's lack of conscience. When he was confronted with facts that revealed his unquestionable guilt, he was brazen enough to deny his obvious fault.

All discipline efforts to squelch Mitchell's behavior had met with limited results at best. His parents had taken away virtually every privilege and prized possession he had. They had spanked him when he refused to cooperate with them. His father even forced Mitchell to wash his mouth with a bar of soap one day after he had caught the boy in a string of consecutive lies. To his dismay, Mitchell had the audacity to tell yet another tale within a couple of hours. Obviously he had failed to grasp the meaning of his punishment.

Mother and Father's patience finally snapped when they learned that their son had been caught in the act of stealing a lawn mower. Mitchell claimed he intended to borrow the mower from a neighbor's garage. His friends said they heard Mitchell brag that he could steal items from others in broad daylight and never get caught. Mom and Dad didn't know what to do with their son. It was obvious to them that the boy had a problem. Not only did they feel confused at how to handle their son's deceit, they could not comprehend the reason for Mitchell's unusual behavior.

Defining the Deceitful Child

Several behaviors are common to the characteristic of deceitfulness. Children and adolescents who exhibit one form of dishonesty almost always display several other related behaviors. The case study of Mitchell typifies how several forms of misbehavior can be tied into one burdensome package of trouble. Intertwined into his behavior pattern were elements of lying, telling half–truths, failure to disclose pertinent details, stealing, exaggerated boasting, and apparent lack of concern for misbehavior.

Though many deceitful children fail to admit to feelings of inferiority or need for recognition, their behavior betrays them as having unmet needs of this kind. Numerous deceitful children do not necessarily have abundant behavior problems. They may seem to be children who are generally compliant and who want to please others.

Other deceitful children display a pattern of dishonesty along with other forms of blatant misbehavior. They also are aggressive toward their peers or argumentative with adults. Their apparent lack of integrity may be a part of a well–established pattern of misconduct.

Lying, stealing, cheating, and related behaviors have different meanings for children at varied age levels. For example, a preschool child may steal from a playmate and then lie about it because he spotted something he wanted and took it. An adolescent may steal and then lie about his behavior in order to gain recognition from his peer group as being daring and bold. The risk of getting caught in the act of deceitfulness increases the thrill of the misbehavior.

Despite the differences seen in the reasons for deceitfulness in individual children and adolescents, several common threads are present that define this child. The more common characteristics are discussed here.

Manipulation hides a deeper insecurity. In our examination of other difficult behavior patterns we have found that manipulation can be used for a variety of reasons. A child may manipulate others as a hidden expression of anger or as a way of stating feelings of dissatisfaction. He may use manipulative tactics to avoid receiving attention. Some children manipulate others simply because they enjoy the feeling of power or control that often follows.

A child may deceive others for any of these reasons but, in most cases, a primary reason for his deceit is to cover a deeper feeling of personal inferiority. Such a ploy serves two purposes in the child's mind: to successfully convince others to view him in an artificially positive light, or to vainly try to convince himself that he is of importance.

One of the more infamous incidents of deceitfulness recorded in the Scripture (Gen. 27:1–46) is Jacob's deception of his father, Isaac, in order to receive his father's blessings as the next head of the household. While Jacob's behavior was motivated by a lust of power and control, there were other contributing factors to his scheme, such as a need to feel important, a desire to be viewed favorably by others, a feeling of vengeance against his brother, and feelings of personal inadequacy that could only be soothed by seizing status.

Unfortunately, deceitful behavior is seldom the route to the completion of any of these goals. Even Jacob struggled with the consequences of damaged family relationships years after his deceptive conduct (Gen. 27:41–46). Manipulative behavior of this sort has a tendency to come back to haunt the child, causing further feelings of inadequacy.

—Case Study—

Albert was a 13–year–old boy who seemed to constantly be at odds with others for trying to present himself in a false light. Others quickly recognized the pitfalls of his claims about himself, but he seemed to be oblivious to his own false mannerisms.

When playing baseball with friends, he had become infamous for arguing over petty interpretations of the children's play. For example, he would claim that an opposing team player was "out" in contrast to all other opinions. He would claim that he was "safe" when he clearly was out—even by the admission of his teammates. He even made up rules to suit his needs, stating that he knew how to follow the guidelines used by professionals.

Albert's manipulative nature did not end when he left the playground. At school he commonly accused classmates of deliberately stealing his completed assignments as a trick against him when in actuality he had not finished the work that he had been given. When asked by his parents if he had schoolwork to complete at home, he denied having homework.

The outward behavior that marked Albert's deceitfulness provided a mask for his real feelings of low self–worth. In comparison to others, he felt that he was not important. He assumed that he was not capable of producing the same good ideas that others were able to do with seeming ease. There was a strong sense of dissatisfaction within him, despite his youth. In short, Albert's behavioral style of deceitfulness had become his awkward way of coping with a deep lack of certainty about his worth as a person. The irony of his deceit was that others, even other children, recognized his manipulative ways as evidence of this personal problem.

Irresponsibility is a pervasive problem. Deceitful behavior is often a part of a larger pattern of irresponsibility. A child may reason that it is simpler to avoid undesirable tasks by the use of fraudulent tactics than to have to give way to responsible behavior. These children are quick to detect chances to take the easy way out of an assigned task and will take advantage of these opportunities.

After a series of successes in these ventures, a pattern of irresponsibility develops.

Irresponsibility and its accompanying deceitfulness can take a variety of forms. Some of the more common practices of irresponsibility include:

- Failure to accept challenges that are within one's range of ability.
- Taking "short cuts" rather than complete a task as was intended.
- Feigning illness or injury as an excuse to avoid expectations of others.
- Offering explanations that confuse rather than clarify.
- Accusing others of breaking the rules or otherwise fouling up matters.
- Failing to complete jobs or assignments.
- Creating diversions that place emphasis on matters other than the task at hand.
- Chronic forgetfulness.
- Procrastination of jobs; persistent promises to "get right on it."
- Failure to work when without direct supervision.
- Coaxing others to do work that has not been assigned to them.
- Claiming ignorance of what was expected.
- Allowing deadlines to pass so it is no longer possible to complete a task.
- Complaining that "no one else has to do it."
- Claiming unfair treatment by others.

Each of these behaviors embraces various forms of deceit. At the root of each form of irresponsibility is a lack of willingness to accept personal accountability for one's actions. The child is quick to point a finger of blame toward another person or circumstance. To do otherwise would expose the child as one involved in fraudulent behavior. The idea of allowing others to plainly view his personal inadequacy paints an undesirable picture for the child.

Communication with others is vague. One of the basic truths about human communication states that all feelings and emotions will be expressed in some fashion. Some emotions are expressed openly to others in verbal form. Others are transmitted by implication through words and actions. The observant person can read between the lines to understand the intended message. Other feelings are expressed through behavior patterns. Even though words are not spoken, the child will give strong clues to how he feels.

A more covert form of communication exists when a child attempts to conceal his true feelings from others. It is necessary to watch the child's actions closely and to carefully consider the words he uses to fully comprehend the child's internal feelings. Without careful observation, the child can experience repeated success in sending distorted, inaccurate messages to others. Such success prevents the child from owning up to the reality he fears.

—Case Study—

Eleven–year–old Tricia had been experiencing normal feelings of admiration for boys for several months. Embarrassed by these feelings, she was quite reluctant to admit her preadolescent fondness for one particular boy. In her own way of thinking, she would rather melt through the floor than confess her affection for boys, especially to her family members. She had, however, shared her secret admiration with her best friend, Sally, thinking the privileged information was safe with her.

One evening Tricia and her friend were playing together at Tricia's house. Tricia's parents and older sister were present as the two girls chatted. Unannounced, Sally broached the forbidden topic and asked Tricia, "Are you and Brad still going together?"

Petrified, Tricia spoke tersely to her playmate, "Of course not! Why would I want to go with him? Just drop it! OK?" Tricia hoped Sally would grasp the seriousness of her request and end the conversation. Sally failed to recognize Tricia's embarrassment.

"What are you talking about Tricia? You told me just yesterday you liked Brad. He likes you, too."

"Just mind your own business, Sally! Why do you always have to act like you know everything?"

Feeling the need to defend Sally, mother interrupted the conversation, "Tricia, it's alright if you like Brad. It's normal for girls your age to be interested in boys."

"Yeah," added Tricia's older sister, "I can remember when I had my first boyfriend. I was embarrassed for anyone to know."

Not at all consoled, Tricia verbally attacked her family members. "Would you two quit talking like that? I don't know what you're talking about. I've never told anyone that I liked Brad or any other boy!" With those words the conversation came to an abrupt halt.

Verbal Statement: **Hidden Message:**

"That's a lie! I don't like Brad!"   *I'm embarrassed to admit I like boys.*

A deceitful child may forcefully deny his feelings through strong verbal statements.

A deceitful pattern of behavior creates a communication dilemma for a child. If he honestly communicates feelings, he draws attention to past efforts to disguise the same or similar feelings. Feeling the need to prevent being exposed as a fraud, the child continues to conceal genuine emotions. As in the case of Tricia, a growing pattern of deceit causes meaningful communication with the child to be difficult at best.

Outward behavior and inner feelings do not match. A defining characteristic that closely resembles the inability to communicate with others is the deceitful child's tendency to display behavior that does not accurately reflect the feelings that are so strongly held within. There is a lack of genuineness in his behavior.

Certainly, children and adolescents cannot be expected to express all they think and feel to each person they encounter. Like adults, young people have a public way of acting that differs from the behavior in the presence of close friends or family members.

Yet unlike the norm that honesty be used when the disclosure of feelings is called for, the deceitful child refuses to reveal his true self, even with those closest to him.

My experience with deceitful young people suggests that there exists a discomfort within these individuals that often is not recognized by others. A frustration builds as the child or teen becomes more deeply entrenched in a phony way of life. If the youngster would express himself honestly, he may make statements resembling the following:

"When I'm at school I hardly ever get into trouble, but at home I'm constantly in a battle with my family. I'm scared others at school will discover what kind of person I really am."

"My friends seem more sure of themselves than I am. If I don't say what they want to hear, they'll know how lost I am."

"I'm not sure what to think about anything. Maybe if I go along with the crowd, I'll eventually decide."

"People have no idea how angry I am inside. If I act like I'm happy, no one will ever find out."

"No one could possibly understand the way I feel. If I told them, they would laugh in disbelief."

The deceitful child assumes that others will take his behavior at face value and will believe that his actions accurately represent his inner self. Those close to the child may recognize, however, that a sharp discrepancy exists between inner feelings and outward behavior. Though each young person has his own favorite methods of deception, some common ways of disguising internal beliefs are as follows:

- Playing the role of an expert or know–it–all.

- Intellectualizing a problem to avoid discussing the emotions involved.

- Laughing inappropriately at people.

- Giving in to peer pressure despite signs of potential harm.

- Refusing to state a belief.

- Overstating a belief.

- Associating only with those in the "elite" crowd.

- Pretending to be interested when there is no interest.

- Working too hard to make a positive impression.

Many young people assume others are being fooled by their deceptive style of behavior. They have confidence that no one will discover the discrepancy between inner feelings and outward behavior. Other youngsters have a growing fear that their deception is readily noticed by all others. But being unwilling to seek verification of those fears, they continue the pattern.

Pride has reached unhealthy levels. Like all other emotional expressions, pride is one that must be maintained in a proper balance. Without a certain amount of pride, the child cannot develop a positive respect for himself. Yet many deceitful individuals have allowed their pride to reach the point that an exaggerated sense of importance is placed on the self.

Pride that has reached unhealthy limits causes a young person to become a high risk for deceitful behavior. Consider how pride can adversely affect a child or adolescent:

- An increased importance is placed on his reputation among his peers.

- Arrogance surfaces as a blanket that covers faults and shortcomings.

- Reactions from others are received with a high level of sensitivity.

- Needs to express true feelings and emotions are ignored.

- Constructive criticism arouses anger rather than causes change.

- Personal weaknesses are not adequately recognized.

- Discomfort arises when others take a leadership position.

Pride that has grown to be too strong causes the child to put on pretenses that suggest all is well within when, in fact, the deceiver is miserable. Ultimately, the young person finds that his excessive pride is not strong enough to cover the unhappiness it brings.

—Case Study—

Odie was a 15–year–old boy who had been involved in a deceitful style of life since his primary years. As a young child, he had not developed a strong feeling of self–importance. On one particular occasion he expressed to me, "I don't remember when I began to pretend I was invincible, but I do recall making a decision to never allow anyone to get close to me because I was afraid I would be hurt. I guess I was disappointed too many times when I was younger because I never seemed to fit in with others."

Odie continued to discuss how pride consumed him. "I can remember making a promise to myself that no one would ever know what I felt inside—not even my parents or my brother. Before you knew it, I could never be counted on to carry out a responsibility. I lied every time I got into a jam. If the facts didn't fit my needs, I would simply make some up. Even when I was caught red–handed in a wrongful act, I'd think of some lame excuse. I simply refused to be honest with anyone."

Odie changed his deceitful strategy when he found himself two grade levels behind his 15–year–old peers. He was on probation with juvenile authorities for shoplifting at a store. He had lost most of his friends and had virtually no one to turn to for help. Even his parents were tired of continually having to bail him out of trouble. Odie realized that his own exaggerated pride and the deceitful life–style it generated were what stood in the way of a more satisfying way of life.

Factors Influencing the Deceitful Child's Behavior

Reactions from others are feared. In response to the question, "Why do you tell lies?" most children will respond that they lie because they do not like what happens to them when they truthfully admit to a wrongdoing. These children fear that they will be scolded, punished, criticized, or embarrassed. In the child's way of thinking, the risk of getting caught is worth the price that would have to be paid if his deceitfulness is discovered.

—Case Study—

Before Derrick came home from school, his school principal called his mother to inform her of some difficulties Derrick had experienced that day. The principal related that the lad had been removed from the school cafeteria because he had taken a classmate's hamburger and spit inside the bun as a crude expression of humor. Later that afternoon, he was disciplined by his classroom teacher for disruptive behavior.

Naturally, Mother was upset upon receiving this news about her son, but thanked the principal for keeping her informed about his behavior. When Derrick walked into the house, Mother greeted him with her normal response.

"Hi, Derrick. How did the day go?"

"Just fine. Same ol' thing at school."

"Nothing special happened today? It was business as usual?" Mother wanted to give Derrick the opportunity to confess his wrongdoings.

"No, Mom! Nothing happened. It was just a plain, ordinary day! Why are you bugging me?"

"I'll tell you why I'm bugging you, young man! Mrs. Lyons called me a little while ago and told me about how you spit on someone's hamburger and how you were rude and disrespectful in your classroom. That's why I'm bugging you. I think you've got some explaining to do! What do you have to say for yourself?" Mother was obviously mad.

"Mom, I was just playing a joke with the hamburger incident. Haven't you ever played a joke on anybody before? And I wasn't being rude in the classroom. That dumb teacher is the one who's rude, but I'll bet Mrs. Lyons forgot to tell you that."

Mother was not satisfied with Derrick's simple explanation of his behavior. "You are not to refer to your teacher as 'dumb.' I'm sure she had plenty of reasons to be upset with you!"

"How do you know, Mother?" Derrick interrupted. "You weren't there! You don't know what she said to me. She told me I was acting like a baby and that she was going to treat me like a baby! Who was being rude? It wasn't me!"

"You probably *were* acting like a baby. In fact, you're not acting very grown-up now. You can just forget about going outside this afternoon. You're restricted to your room until bedtime. That ought to give you plenty of time to think about what you've done today!"

Still complaining, Derrick went to his room and slammed the door. Mother sat down in the living room wondering what could be done to change her son's bad habits.

Certainly Derrick had a need to be held accountable for the inappropriate way he behaved at school. Mother's hope was to leave an opportunity available for the boy to admit his wrongdoing so he could accept his punishment and learn a lesson from his mistake. Instead, Derrick chose to be deceitful and to hide the fact that he had committed a wrongful act at school. Even when his mother revealed that she was aware of his misbehavior, he refused to admit his guilt. Instead, he claimed he was simply being playful and that his teacher was the cause of his disrespect. The response he received from his mother actually increased the likelihood that he would continue to engage in deceitful activity.

Consider the reactions Derrick was given that encouraged him to refrain from honesty:

- The conversation began with a trap as Derrick was asked a casual question to which he gave a casual reply. After pressing him for the "right" answer, he was emotionally leveled by the evidence mother had collected.

- The presentation of evidence that Derrick had been deceitful was expressed with much anger. Derrick had likely been the recipient of this undesirable reaction before. His failure to tell the truth marked a futile attempt to avoid another of his mother's outbursts.

- Derrick's unconcerned attitude as he explained his behavior was not enough to satisfy his mother. She wanted him to express regret for his misconduct. But, Derrick quickly realized that to be sorrowful would then allow his mother an opportunity to further belabor the point that he had shown poor judgment. Not wishing to sit through further chastising, he chose to ignore the problem.

- When Derrick referred to his teacher as "dumb" and "rude," his mother gave him an implied message that he was not permitted to feel as he did. Not wanting to abandon his own convictions, he became defensive and argued for his right to disagree with his teacher's tactics.

- By telling Derrick, "You probably were acting like a baby," and then elaborating further on that theme, Mother was using a name–calling technique that reduced her son's feelings of self–importance as a person. With this emphasis on his personal character rather than his behavior, the likelihood that Derrick would want to express himself in an honest fashion was reduced.

- Punishment of Derrick encouraged him to surmise that dishonesty could be used to his benefit. As he considered matters, he assumed that if his mother did not know of his future misbehavior, perhaps he could avoid the inevitable restrictions that were to follow. In his mind, the risk of being caught was one he was willing to take in order to avoid certain discipline.

  To determine why a negative behavior pattern of any type persists, it is helpful to observe the events following that undesirable behavior. In the case of the deceitful child, deceitfulness is often followed by an attempt to avoid being caught in the act and held accountable. The fear of a negative response, then, motivates the child to continue in a self–defeating pattern of behavior. The helpful intentions of the parents can become an unintentional contributing factor to deceitfulness.

Deception may successfully result in attention from others. Because the deceptive child typically harbors feelings of personal inadequacy, he is in constant need of reassurance from others that he is an important person. Positive attention from others provides a child the most common security that he is a person of value.

Yet, the deceptive child feels shortchanged in the amount of positive attention he receives. He then develops an image of himself that is mostly negative. He assumes that he is not important because others do not consistently affirm his value. The negative cycle of deception that can evolve from these feelings of low self–worth usually results in one of two behavior patterns.

Desiring attention from others, the child goes to far–reaching excesses to achieve that goal. However, his negative manner of seeking attention is an overstatement of his need for approval. The child's deep hope is that his parent will recognize his cry for help and provide relief in the form of increased individual contact. Unfortunately, the end result most often involves some form of negative reaction and a failure on the part of the adult to correctly interpret the behavior as a statement of need.

An additional reason the child displays deception is found in his need to know where he stands in the eyes of others. Feeling poorly about himself, he wants to know if others feel that way about him. As if testing others, the child acts in a dishonest way, closely observing the reaction he is given. If the reaction is negative, the child's feelings of inadequacy are confirmed. If little comment or inference is made about his inadequacy as a person, the child has the opportunity to reevaluate his poor self–esteem. In most cases though, deception is not the route for most children to successfully solicit assurance that they are of worth as people.

—Case Study—

Debra was a nine–year–old child whom her parents and teachers described as untrustworthy. She commonly told lies, frequently stole from others, and failed to learn from the discipline used on her. She was brought to my office so I could determine her personal needs and suggest the best method to meet those needs.

I found Debra to be candid in discussing her own dishonest habits. She freely told me that she "lied all the time." She explained that she had stolen money from her mother's purse, taken items from her sister's room without permission, and even smuggled inexpensive objects out of stores. When confronted by others, she denied any wrongdoing.

Focusing on Debra's opinion of herself, it was obvious that she did not hold herself in high esteem. Feeling that she was unimportant in comparison to others, she felt left out of the mainstream of childhood activity. Her explanation of how she drifted into a deceptive behavior pattern provided a typical portrait of how unmet needs for attention can contribute to negative actions.

"I don't want others to dislike me, but they do anyway. People say I lie a lot. I do lie, but they don't understand why."

"You must have a good reason for lying to others. Can you tell me what that reason is?" I asked.

"People don't pay attention to me very much. But if I'm in trouble, everybody pays a lot of attention to me."

"That's a simple reason. You do dishonest things so people will notice you, but when they do notice you they probably fuss at you or punish you."

"Yeah, I get grounded all the time, but I guess that's because I deserve to be punished because I'm always doing something wrong."

In a cyclical fashion, Debra had become caught up in a pattern of behavior that constantly resulted in negative consequences. Feeling the need for recognition, she took the risk that others would correctly interpret her hidden request for attention and provide for it. Instead, she received affirmation that she *was* the negative person she believed herself to be. With that acknowledgement, she then became more likely to continue in a self–defeating cycle.

Pressure to succeed can encourage deception. The word *pressure* has many bothersome implications, especially for children and adolescents. When a child feels pressure from others to meet a given standard, an urgency develops that causes the young person to want relief from the stress and strain he feels.

Along with this sense of need to ease the burden of pressure, the child may find himself acting in a deceitful manner. He becomes something he is not in order to more quickly release himself from his troubles. But when individuals choose shortcuts to deal with big problems, the result is often the addition of even more burdens. The continual presence of pressure, then, contributes to a cyclical pattern of deceiving others. The pressures that the younger child faces are different than those confronting the teenager. Pressure to be "successful" as a person exists at any age. I have developed a list of the primary pressures that confront children who are preteen and a separate detailing of those stresses that more keenly affect teenagers. Too much pressure at either of these age levels can encourage deceitfulness. The most common pressures facing the preteen include:

- The desire to meet the expectations of significant adults, especially parents.

- Making and keeping one or two close friendships with other children.

- Doing well in competitive settings, including school, organized athletics, artistic activities, etc.

- The desire to develop personal independence accompanied by a fear of being forced to be independent.

- A growing resentment toward authority.

- The desire to fit in with the peer group (with increased age).

- The introduction to a seemingly endless number of new situations, e.g., going to school, staying home alone for short periods of time, spending the night away from home, etc.

- Jealousy of siblings or of other children.

- Confronting childhood fears, e.g., being alone, sleeping in the dark, speaking in front of others.

- The need for assurance from others, especially family members.

There are certainly other sources of pressure confronting the younger child, but these represent the most commonly expressed sources of concern. Most of the pressures facing the child are under at least some degree of control from the family. Certainly, the world beyond the family has an influence on the child. During the adolescent years, the family's influence subsides in favor of the pressures of the world, even though the family can continue to exert pressure on the child (either positively or negatively). The most common pressures of adolescence that contribute to a deceptive pattern of behavior include:

- The overwhelming desire to meet the expectations of peers.

- The temptation to experiment because "everybody else is doing it," e.g., alcohol, drugs, sex.

- Being included in a group that is recognized as prestigious.

- Feelings of confusion that accompany the search for identity.

- Increased criticism of adults who are in positions of authority.

- The desire for greater financial independence.

- Learning to interact with members of the opposite sex.

- Heightened awareness of social issues.

- Increased desire to accumulate material items.

- Having to make important choices about the future.

These pressures can cause the teenager to become focused too heavily on his own needs and to neglect the needs of others. Few parents of adolescents have avoided the exasperation that accompanies their child's awkward attempts to successfully respond to the pressures of the world. The teen often becomes self–centered (see Chapter 5) to the point that a healthy objectivity toward life is lost. Deceit becomes a tempting way of skirting the demands of the family, peer group, and society. Not able to foresee the long–range negative results of such behavior, the adolescent proceeds in this undesirable mode hoping to ease the pressures he feels.

Leniency can encourage deceitfulness. I know a man who once boasted to me that he was a close friend of the district attorney in a rural Texas county. Because of this friendship, he explained, he could drive his car at any rate of speed he desired in that county because he could call upon his friend to "take care" of any speeding ticket he might receive.

When I first heard about this man's arrangement with his pal, the district attorney, I thought he was lucky. On further thought, I realized that the deceit this man was allowed to exercise likely gave him the feeling that such behavior could be exhibited in other situations as well. The continued practice of dishonesty would eventually catch the man off guard and result in an unexpected dose of humiliation.

Like the man with the license to speed, many young people are given the message that deceitfulness is ordained simply because too few boundaries are provided, giving the child no sense of obligation to others. Having learned that little is expected of him by his family, the child incorrectly assumes that others will also overlook his shortcomings. Confrontation with authority figures who demand accountability results in efforts to deceive those persons. Deception can become a means of maintaining a mis-guided life–style free from demands and expectations.

In most instances, the lenient parent is hopeful that the child will be appreciative of his tolerance and will demonstrate that appreciation by acting in a responsible manner. All too often, the child recognizes his parents' lenient behavior as the very chance he needs to act irresponsibly without fear of being called on to explain himself.

Examples of how children may develop deceitfulness as a result of too much leniency are as follows:

- A junior–high–aged adolescent who has persistent difficulty in math routinely calls upon a friend for help in completing homework assignments. These telephone sessions usually result in the friend providing answers to the homework problems. Though the child does not understand the concepts behind the homework assignment, she maintains good grades because of her friend's help. The girl's parents do not believe that their daughter is cheating and are glad she has the initiative to do what it takes to successfully complete her homework.

- A father takes his 13–year–old son to a ball game. Not want-ing to pay an extra $2.50 for his son's ticket, the father purchases a ticket for children who are 12 years old or younger. Handing the ticket to the boy, the parent chuckles and com-ments, "You *are* still 12 years old, aren't you?"

- A neighbor complains to a father that his son has been throw-ing the weeds from their yard over the fence into his yard. The father perceives the neighbor as being the type who constantly has a complaint. Because of his own desire to avoid cooperating with a grouchy neighbor, the father chooses to ignore the man's request and does not mention the complaint to the son.

- A mother overhears her daughter talking on the telephone to a friend. Her daughter is laughing about an incident in which she and her friend successfully humiliated another girl by spreading rumors about that girl's antics with a boy who has a bad reputation. Because the mother never really liked the girl who has been slandered, she overlooks the matter and even finds amusement in the incident.

In virtually all the cases, the display of leniency with a child certainly is not a deliberate attempt to teach that child deceitfulness. Even though the intent of leniency is to overlook what appears to be a minor problem, its cumulative effect over time may be to encourage behavior by the child that fails to recognize the need for honesty. A pattern of irresponsibility can be fueled by the successful avoidance of accountability that deceitfulness sometimes brings.

Managing the Deceitful Child

Management of deceitfulness in a child must focus on two areas of concern. The first concern is the deceitful behavior itself. A response must be given to the child to discourage dishonesty and encourage truthfulness. Secondly, and more importantly, the underlying reasons for the child's deceit must be addressed. To focus strictly on misbehavior rather than its underlying causes creates a sense of frustration and misunderstanding within the child that encourages him to repeat his maladjusted behavior.

In discussing the management of the deceitful child, we must deal with how to confront his misbehavior, but greater emphasis will be placed on attacking, in a positive manner, the problems that so often underlie this behavior pattern. Greater success can be achieved by erasing the child's need to resort to negative tactics as a way of stating underlying needs.

Encourage honesty through open communication. Many children tell lies because they are afraid of what will happen if they tell the truth. Once I have gotten to know a deceitful child fairly well, I frequently ask him to explain the *real* reason for his dishonesty. Some children will show their distrust in others by failing to be honest about why they are dishonest! But, many of these young people freely talk about the verbal response they fear they will receive from their parent (or other adult) if they *do* tell the truth.

Surprisingly, the deceitful child is less concerned about the punishment he may receive. He is more concerned about the possibility that he may be reacted to in a way that will create feelings of shame and embarrassment within himself. Or the child may share how the response he receives sends a message that he is inadequate as a person.

Emotionally charged communication from an adult to a deceitful child suggests to the child that the adult has a problem. As the child perceives things, the adult's problem is that of having to deal with a dishonest child. Instead of feeling encouraged to be truthful, the child who is confronted by an angry parent will continue his deceit to prevent even more anger from being directed toward him. Of course, this tactic frequently fails, leaving the child in a perpetual predicament.

To encourage the child to focus more on the responsibility he has for his own deceitfulness, it is important that the parent curb the urge to react emotionally to the child's expression of his thoughts and feelings. An objective understanding of the child's need to conclude for himself the way he should handle life's problems is a first step in developing a more open communication pattern. The parent must believe that the child is capable of moving in a positive direction in the decisions he makes. The parent acts as a guide for the child as the young person develops his own approach to life.

—Case Study—

Rex returned to his mother's house following a weekend visit with his father who had been divorced from Rex's mother for several years. Rex felt that he was in a continual bind with his father because of his father's insistence on banning any conversation that mentioned Rex's mother. As the father viewed it, the time Rex spent with him was not to be used talking about a woman he no longer loved.

Rex was confused about how to respond to his father's request to avoid comments about his mother. He loved his father and wanted to comply with his request, yet an uneasy feeling inside told him there was nothing wrong about conversation concerning his mother. He could not talk to his father about the matter, but decided that following this visit with his father, he would discuss his dilemma with his mother.

"Mom," Rex began hesitantly, "there's something I don't understand about Dad. When I'm at his house, he doesn't like me to mention your name. I try not to, but sometimes I want to tell him about something that you and I did, so I do. Then he either ignores me or changes the subject."

Focusing on Rex's need to express himself and not her own internal reaction, Mom responded. "I'm sure it's difficult to avoid talking about the things you do with me. You want your dad to know all about the activities you are involved in."

"I do, but Dad doesn't want to hear about it. He says that we don't need to talk about what happens at your house since you and he aren't married anymore."

"That keeps you from sharing a lot of things you'd like to share."

"Why is Dad like that, anyway? Why can't I just talk about anything I want to discuss? It's dumb to say I can't mention your name in his house!"

"That rule doesn't make much sense to you, does it?"

"No . . . I don't know if Dad will ever change. It makes it hard for me to talk to him about anything." With these words the conversation tapered with little further comment from Mom.

In this dialogue between mother and son, honesty in expression was achieved. Rex talked of the confused feelings he had about his father's unwritten rule to avoid conversation about Rex's mother. He was met with responses that indicated understanding of his dilemma, but which left the burden of responsibility on Rex to conclude what he would do about his father.

The dialogue between Rex and his mother could have been quite different, however, if Mom had chosen to become too emotionally invested in her son's problem. On hearing Rex's initial statement about his father's preference not to talk of his former wife, Mom could have blurted out her own opinion of Rex's father. She could have exclaimed in heated terms her disgust for the man and her disrespect for his poor judgment. Or she might have chosen to be overly sympathetic with Rex in an attempt to lure him into disdaining his father.

Any response from Mom that was laced with her own emotion would have had the effect of removing from Rex the responsibility of reaching a conclusion about Dad's policy. Mother could have taken the responsibility upon herself and decided for Rex what his opinion of his father should be. The result would have been frustration on Rex's part that he had been prevented from expressing himself in a complete manner.

The opportunity a child has to communicate freely with others is a major detractor of deceitfulness. The child who cannot talk openly about his thoughts and feelings is more likely to drift into more subtle, often negative methods of expression. The child whose parent allows him to maintain responsibility for his opinions and feelings is more likely to develop a pattern of honest communication that is free from deceit.

Avoid emotional reactions that hurt. Confrontation is a common reaction to a child who has displayed dishonesty. Paul tells parents to avoid provoking anger in a child, while at the same time providing proper discipline and instruction (Eph. 6:4). When a child has acted deceitfully, the parent wants an explanation for that wrong behavior. In the process of seeking information, the parent can slip away from Paul's guidance into patterns of communication that do harm to the relationship with the child, encouraging further deceit by that young person. Examined below are some of the more common communication pitfalls that should be avoided.

- *Outbursts of anger.* Angry outbursts result from a parent's intense feeling of frustration. The usual intent of this explosion of words is to cause the child to feel so badly about his deceitful behavior that it will not be repeated. Yet, the child often feels sufficiently negative about himself that the verbal tongue-lashing serves to convince him that positive behavior is not expected of him. The child may tell himself, "I can't do anything right." Outbursts of anger also set the stage for a bitter war of words with the child.

- *Threats.* Many threats are begun with the phrase, "If you don't . . . ." A deceitful child will often recognize a threat as a challenge. A threat is perceived by the child as a promise the parent does not want to have to fulfill. Some children see threatening statements as an opportunity for thrills and excitement. A threat will be challenged just to see if further problems can be created for the parent. Rather than employ threats to diminish irresponsible behavior patterns, firm guidelines should be announced, immediately followed by decisive action.

- *Public comments.* One of the most damaging ways to break down communication with a child is for that child to learn that his misbehavior has been made public. Whether the child is present when negative statements are made, or he hears from other sources that his dishonest actions have been publicly revealed, the child is immeasurably hurt. A variety of conclusions may be made by the child. He may think, *So that's what my parents expect of me*, or, *You can't trust adults with any personal information*, or, *I'll get even with them for talking about me*, or, *They're telling it all wrong*, or, *My parents don't think very highly of me.* Whatever the child's conclusion of his parent's public statements about his indiscretion, there is little doubt that the result will be further deceitfulness.

- *Why questions.* I often ask children and teenagers to explain their negative reaction to parental questions that begin with the word *why.* One particularly deceitful boy told me, "If my parents don't know why I do the things I do, I'm sure not going to give away any secrets." Another boy told me, "My mom will ask me why I did something and before I can answer, she'll tell me why I did it. I think she just wants to start an argument." A teenaged girl candidly stated, "When my parents ask why, I always say 'I don't know.' I love to see them get mad when I say that."

| **Parent:** | **Child:** |
| "Why did you do that?" | "I don't know." |

Claiming ignorance can allow a child to continue a deceitful pattern of communication.

I recommend that parents avoid *Why* questions since the only person who can provide the desired answer is their deceitful child. If his pattern of deceit holds true, an honest response is not likely. Decisive action should be taken based on the parent's unique knowledge of the child and the best available information about the incident in question. The parent need not assume a "detective's" role in determining why a behavior was exhibited. To do so gives unnecessary control to the child.

- *The silent treatment.* Saying nothing at all can speak volumes to a deceitful child who knows that his parent's silence is backed by an anger that is not verbalized. I've known many a child who quivers when his parent gives the silent treatment. The child may interpret this communication gesture as evidence that he is so bad his mother and father cannot bring themselves to make a comment. He may feel that his parents think so lowly of him that he is not worth talking to. He may also learn that when he, too, experiences an emotional reaction, it is advantageous to hold it in.

  The preferred response to the deceitful child is to briefly state an honest emotion, provide the necessary behavioral limit, and then resume a normal pattern of communication as soon as possible. Use of the silent treatment serves only to prolong a problem and create new opportunities for dishonest exchanges between parent and child.

Take action based on the information that is available. One of the tactics the deceitful child frequently uses is that of creating confusion. If he can keep his parents guessing about what really happened, then it will be virtually impossible for the adult to know with certainty what the child's role was in a given incident.

This tactic of creating confusion places control in the hands of the child and can provide him with enough success in avoiding accountability that a trend emerges. It is the role of the parent, not the child, to be in control of disciplinary matters. For the child to be in control will result in the creating of a pattern of behavior that is not in the child's long-term best interests.

The parent must be able to objectively view the behavior of the child and decide the action he feels is necessary to discourage further deceitfulness. A lack of cooperation from the child should not result in no decision from the parent because of lack of concrete evidence. There are times that the parent must rely on his knowledge of the child's tendencies and upon parental "hunches" as a guide in decision–making.

—Case Study—

The Stafford family had a garden in their backyard. Planting and harvesting vegetables was a family project that even the children participated in. Though the experience of watching plants grow to maturity was enjoyable, the children were less than enthusiastic when the time came to pick the vegetables.

One summer morning, Mrs. Stafford asked her two daughters to pick green beans from the garden while she worked on other tasks in the house. With frowns on their faces, the girls began their work in the garden. Because of their lack of enthusiasm, a poor job of harvesting was done. Many beans were left on the vines.

When the girls returned, their mother asked if they had completed their job. The girls replied affirmatively. Mrs. Stafford knew that many more beans were ready for harvesting than the girls had picked.

"Girls, I'm sure there are more beans than these to be picked. I'd like you to go back outside and finish the job."

The girls complained simultaneously, "But Mom, that's all we saw. There aren't any more!"

"Girls, please don't argue with me. I'd like you to go back to the garden and finish picking the beans." With those words she went about her own work. Grumbling, the girls went outside again to resume their work.

In this simple example of deceitful behavior by two sisters, we can see the way in which the parent must maintain control of the decisions to be made regarding the management of that deceitfulness. As a part of their ploy to avoid working, the sisters worked in a half–hearted manner and failed to fulfill their assigned job. They then attempted to present their harvest as the completion of their duty.

Mrs. Stafford was aware of her daughters' lack of enthusiasm and their tendency to claim completion of work that was far short of complete. She also knew that the amount of beans in their bucket was less than what was ready to be picked.

Coupling the information available to her with the knowledge of her daughters' tendencies, Mother took action. She sent the girls back to the garden to complete their job. The girls' complaints and insistence that there were no more beans to be picked were ignored.

It is important to note the reactions that Mrs. Stafford refrained from giving to her daughters. She did not argue with the girls about whether or not all the beans had been picked. Confident that she was correct in her assumption that many beans were left behind, she focused on her need to provide parental leadership to her daughters and not upon a debate about the number of ripened beans in the garden. To have argued could have given the girls at least momentary control of the situation.

Mrs. Stafford also refused to use negative adjectives to describe her daughters. She could have referred to them as *lazy*, or *irresponsible*, or *unconcerned*. She even could have accused them of lying to her. Avoiding statements that would attack the girls' self-esteem, she chose only to deal with the problem at hand. Reference to the girls' character was not needed.

The girls' mother also could have chosen to use sarcasm such as, "Do you expect me to believe you picked all the beans in the garden? You've got to be kidding!" Yet, such a display of a lack of regard for her daughters' dignity would have increased their lack of desire to cooperate with her.

The role of the parent, as demonstrated by Mrs. Stafford, is to assume control of a situation in which a child has exhibited deceit. Action is to be taken based on the best information available. While the child's dignity should be upheld, he should not be allowed to slip into negative behavior patterns that will not serve him well as he grows older.

The consequence should match the crime. There is probably little that raises the ire of a parent more than deception at the hands of a child. The strong urge of the parent is often to strike with force in a way that communicates to the child that such behavior is completely unacceptable.

While it is certainly necessary for the child to be held accountable for his deceitful behavior, it must be kept in mind that the role of the parent is to respond to the child in a way that will increase the likelihood that similar behaviors will not reoccur.

Keep in mind the fact that children exhibit deceitfulness in part because of their fear of what might happen to them if the truth were known. The parent should avoid the use of heavy punishments as a way of reducing dishonesty. Our knowledge of the deceitful child tells us that his deceitfulness will continue if being honest results in severe punishment.

—Case Study—

Chris, a fifth–grade student, was dishonest in telling his parents that he had been completing all his homework over the past few weeks. But, to the parents' chagrin, they eventually learned that their child had lied to them about his study habits. His poor grades on his report card provided strong evidence that he was doing little homework.

The first impulse of Chris' parents was to provide strong punishment in an effort to impress upon the boy the serious nature of his offense. Yet, through reason, the parents determined that to punish Chris would only push him farther away from them since they would then become Chris' adversaries. Instead of punishing Chris, they recognized that the most effective way of dealing with his deceitfulness and its accompanying lack of responsibility was to draw tighter limits around him in regard to his schoolwork.

The parents realized that by having little contact with Chris' teachers, they had not provided their son with a system of accountability for his schoolwork. It had become relatively easy for him to lapse into irresponsible work habits and then to lie when asked how he was doing in keeping his responsibilities.

A conference was called with Chris' teachers. A plan was developed to provide more frequent contact between parents and teacher as well as the opportunity for Chris to convince his parents that he was completing his classroom work. In this way, Chris' parents could provide order to his schedule, requiring him to complete homework assignments before engaging in more enjoyable activities.

A part of the plan of action called for Mom and Dad to discuss with Chris their intended method of dealing with his problem. He was told, "Chris, this past six weeks we were unaware that you had not been completing all your assignments at school. We are not pleased with your poor grades. We have met with your teachers and have developed a plan in which they will send home a progress report each Friday afternoon informing us of the assignments you have completed and those you have not. We will provide you time to finish any unfinished work before you participate in any of your weekend activities. Once your work is completed, you are free to do as you please."

The parents went on to tell Chris that should new guidelines be required to prevent him from further irresponsibility, such action would be immediately taken. Throughout their discussion with him they refrained from the use of threats, expressions of disgust, a show of anger, and other communication forms that would focus on Chris' negative character traits. Emphasis was placed solely on the resolution of a behavior pattern that required adjustment.

The application of a system of behavior management that causes deceitfulness to work against a child allows him to assume greater responsibility for his own actions. The burden of improving his own lot rests squarely on the child's shoulders. By drawing more restrictive behavioral boundaries and avoiding the potential power struggles that frequently come about when a child feels threatened by punishment, the parent is able to be more objective in his role with the child. The adult is then freed to place more emphasis on developing a positive bond with the child.

Work on developing a stronger self–image. As has already been described, deceitfulness is often an awkward attempt by the child to let others know that something inside feels wrong. Unable to adequately describe his emotions, the child or adolescent hopes others will be perceptive enough to recognize his deception as a futile attempt to solicit help for a wounded self–image. Unfortunately, the child's way of communicating his emotions through inappropriate behavior too often draws excessive attention to the misbehavior and not enough attention to the underlying emotional need.

Because of their advanced age and experience, parents must be quick to respond to the root of a behavior problem rather than expend excessive energy on the behavior itself. The most important elements of a discipline plan are implemented when a child is *not* engaged in a wrongful act. Activities and communication with the child that cause him to feel a strong sense of worth about himself prevent that child from relying upon deceptive ways of expressing his emotional needs.

I like to view the child as being something like a sponge. The young person has a tendency to absorb feelings and beliefs about his worth as an individual based on the way others, especially family members, talk to him and act toward him. The child asks himself questions such as, "How do other people feel about me?" "How important am I to others?" "How competent am I?" He receives answers to these questions from those whose opinions he values the most—his family members, and especially his parents.

A parent can show positive feelings to his child by:

- Verbally affirming that the child is important.

- Making an effort to spend time with the child individually at least several times per week.

- Touching the child with a hug, arm around the shoulder, or friendly nudge.

- Telling the child "I love you" regularly.

- Sending nonverbal messages through pleasant facial expressions.

- Verbally recognizing his worth before others.

A parent can demonstrate to the child that he is important by:

- Fulfilling promises that were previously made.

- Being on time to activities the child is involved in.

- Engaging in play activities or informal talk with the child.

- Providing undivided attention when the child has something to say.

- Meeting a child on his "turf" (e.g., listen as he practices his piano lessons, or watch him as he practices for a play).

- Asking the child's opinion on a matter.

- Refraining from denying the child's right to express an opposing point of view.

A parent can tell the child he is competent by:

- Providing specific information about the value of a task well done (e.g., "Thanks for taking your dishes to the sink. That makes my job simpler.").

- Congratulating the child for correcting a mistake.

- Charting the child's progress in any area and commenting on it.

- Allowing the child to make a decision the whole family follows.

- Assigning tasks that the child is able to successfully complete.

- Asking the child to describe an event or give instructions to you or to another person.

Of course, the list of ways a parent can enhance a child's self-esteem can go on to include many other similar parent responses. The child who receives abundant reassurance that he has value will feel more open toward others. The need for him to disguise his insecurity will diminish while, simultaneously, his desire to cooperate will increase.

Summary

Deceitful behavior is characterized by a variety of outward expressions that have in common the element of evasiveness. Deceitful behavior can be displayed by children who are not overtly disturbed, but it can also serve as a warning signal that more deeply rooted emotional problems are present in the child. Deceitfulness has several characteristics that are commonly found in children who frequently engage in this practice. The more common characteristics include:

- Manipulation that hides a deeper insecurity.

- A pattern of irresponsible behavior.

- Vague communication with others.

- A mismatch between inner feelings and outward behavior.

- An unhealthy sense of self–pride.

Deceitful behavior is frequently influenced by the response a child receives from others. This behavior pattern often is a way for the child to make a statement about his own fears and needs. Influences which can contribute to a deceitful pattern of behavior include:

- A fear of how others will respond to him.

- A need for increased attention from others.

- Pressure from others to act in a specific manner.

- Parental leniency.

Effective management of deceitfulness involves more than simply responding to the child with disciplinary action. While the deceitful child must certainly recognize that he will be held accountable for his behavior, it is vital to also address the symptoms that are at the root of the young person's dishonesty. Elimination of the need for the child to show his discontent through covert misbehavior will result in a healthier way of relating to others. Guidelines for managing the deceitful child include:

- Development of a family communication pattern that is marked by openness.

- Avoidance of the use of emotion–laden responses that cause harm to the parent–child relationship.

- Parental decisiveness that calls upon the adult to take corrective action based on the best available information.

- Consequences that are appropriate to the deceitful act that allow the child to focus more fully on his need to develop responsible behavior.

- Efforts to improve the self–image of the child.

Session 1

Study Session Objective:
To recognize factors that influence deceitfulness in children.

Biblical Reference: Gen. 27:1–46
Read of Jacob's deception of his father. Notice the cumulative effect of Jacob's deceitfulness in the relationships of his family members.

Discussion Questions:
1. How does the deceitful child set himself up for continual failure in his relationships? Do most adults recognize the cyclical pattern of this child's behavior?

2. What communication patterns can parents and children engage in that encourage rather than discourage deceitfulness?

3. What emotional burdens would a deceitful child have to carry as a result of his own behavior? How does this shape his self-esteem?

4. What role does the need for control play in the development of deceitfulness? How do deceitfulness and oppositional behavior relate to one another?

5. Are all deceitful children oppositional? How can a young person who is not rebellious by nature be pushed into this form of misbehavior? Does that make him an oppositional child?

Assignments:
1. Take a poll of your children. Tell them you want constructive feedback from them about some of the things you say and do that prevent them from talking openly with you. Don't challenge their statements or offer your defense. Listen carefully.

2. Think of some of the excuses your child has used as a way of avoiding responsibility. Notice the creativity involved in many of these excuses. Use this exercise as a way of learning to emotionally detach yourself from your child's deceitful activity.

Session 2

Study Session Objective:

To learn to diminish the effects of your child's deceitfulness and thus decrease its likelihood.

Biblical Reference: Gal. 6:3–5, 7–10

Paul, the apostle, tells of the unfortunate consequences of self–deception. Make it your aim to lead your family into a communication pattern that emphasizes honesty.

Discussion Questions:

1. How can a deceitful child become "hooked" on a behavior pattern of dishonesty? What factors make it difficult for him to change this cycle of behavior?

2. What are ways you can provide attention to your child that will discourage him from resorting to deceitful activity?

3. What personal characteristics do you display that may cause your child to feel you are overbearing? Is it your intention to encourage your child to be less than honest? Do you have good intentions as a parent that are carried too far?

4. How quick are you to step in and attempt to force a solution on one of your child's problems? How does your child interpret your actions?

5. Who makes the decisions in your home? Does your child indicate through word or action that he would like a stronger voice in decisions regarding him? What would happen if your child was allowed greater latitude in the choices he makes?

Assignments:

1. Think of some of the rewards you received as a child from your parents. Think further of some of the rewards you wish you had received. Apply these thoughts to your child this week as you interact with him.

2. Evaluate the degree to which you allow your child to make decisions. If you are too lenient, take a stronger stand on a

specific issue this week. If you are too stringent, be willing to compromise. Your child may be able to tell you which type of family leader you are.

7

There's Hope for Your Family—

Words of Encouragement

Things Never Stay the Same

Every summer my family and I enjoy swimming at a pool we have gone to for years. We have friends we see during the summer that we seldom see between Labor Day and Memorial Day. Each summer as families renew friendships, comments are inevitably made about the way in which our children have grown and changed. That annual ackowledgement continues to remind me that things never stay the same. Within each of our families, the process of change is ongoing.

Regardless of the personal characteristics of your child, he is constantly changing. While you cannot alter his personality, you can offer positive experiences that may have a decisive effect on your child's personal, emotional, and spiritual progress through life.

In the same way that children change as they mature, parents change as they go through their own maturation as adults. We learn from the experiences we have with our family members and can make adjustments according to the knowledge and wisdom we have acquired through our daily encounters. As the leader of the family, it is your position to start the healing process that can lead to a more fulfilling life for your child.

—Case Study—

I had seen the Jenkins family 15–20 times over the course of two years. This family first came to me because their son, Randy, who was 12 at the time, was increasingly confused about his position within his peer group. He was a child who experienced many of the emotional qualities that have been discussed in this book. He was sensitive and caring to the point that others took advantage of him. He worried constantly about how others perceived him and questioned his sense of self–worth regularly.

Randy's parents had tried to help him by making suggestions and offering solutions to his social problems. They could not understand why their son repeatedly rejected their offers of help. They were frustrated with him. Randy felt even more exasperation than his parents, complaining that they did not understand him or appreciate the emotions he was experiencing.

Through the course of time, Mr. and Mrs. Jenkins learned to adjust their communication with Randy. They helped him to feel more completely understood, but allowed him to maintain ultimate responsibility for the conclusions he came to about himself and his peer problems.

Although Randy had previously complained that his parents did not understand him, his initial response to their accepting form of communication was fear. While he felt relieved that his parents understood him, there was a helpless feeling that accompanied the realization that he could no longer rely on his parents to take full responsibility for his emotional needs.

Convinced that they needed to go along with the changes suggested in our counseling sessions, Mr. and Mrs. Jenkins remained firm in their commitment to look at life from Randy's point of view. As time passed, Randy began to feel more comfortable with himself. The heart–to–heart talks he had with his parents became more frequent as well as more productive.

At age 14, a more confident Randy was able to tell me, "I'm doing a lot better job of getting along with my friends. I've quit trying to fit in with the 'in group' and I'm doing more things with other kids I really enjoy being with."

As Randy and I talked about his relationship with his parents, he told me, "My Mom and Dad still worry about me and sometimes try too hard to tell me what I should do. But, I can talk a lot better with them now because they listen to me. I used to feel that no matter what I said, they didn't understand me. Now I know that even though they still worry about me, they really do accept me. I've quit fighting with them as much because now I don't have to argue or shout to get my point across to them."

The change that took place within the Jenkins family was a result of changes made in both Randy and his parents. Mr. and Mrs. Jenkins started the change cycle by adjusting their parental reactions to their son's emotional needs. They allowed Randy to accept responsibility for his progress. As he matured in age, he also matured in his understanding of himself. He was then able to be more comfortable with himself and adjusted his social expectations to his personal strengths and weaknesses.

Know When to Ask for Help

I was recently interviewed by a college student who was working on a term paper for a class. He had chosen to write about the daily practice of a psychologist. One of his questions dealt with the greatest frustrations of being a psychologist. I explained that perhaps the greatest frustration in my job is in knowing that many good families wait until a problem situation in their family reaches a crisis point before they seek help.

I am often asked by parents for guidance in knowing when to pursue counseling for the family or for a troubled young person. The following guidelines are offered:

- You, as a parent, can trust your own instinctive feelings. If you feel uncomfortable about the direction of your child's behavior or the potential effect of your reaction to your child, professional counsel could be useful to you. It is often possible that a psychologist may offer appropriate guidance that can provide immediate relief before a problem becomes too difficult to endure.

- If your child's behavior suggests he is emotionally uncomfortable, intervention may be required. Although many children and teenagers are fearful of the suggestion to visit a helping professional, a positive experience at the hands of a seasoned psychologist can be rewarding to the young person. An understanding professional can encourage hope in a child or teenager by displaying understanding and giving positive direction for change in the family.

- If your emotions have become hard for you to control as you deal with your child, you have, no doubt, questioned if there is a better way to positively influence your child's growth. A psychologist's ability to offer insight into your emotional struggles can have positive effects that offer you relief.

I view counseling as more than just an opportunity to talk with someone who encourages good feelings. The counseling process is an educational process. Through the counseling experience a family can learn of the strengths and weaknesses of each family member. Communication needs can be identified and enhanced. Emotional support for one another can become a foundation for a closeness that brings the family together.

There are times in which family members must consider more serious forms of treatment that may include hospitalization. The need for inpatient care is typically reserved for situations in which the child, or even adults, may require intensive work to overcome emotional, behavioral, and spiritual conflicts. Situations that could call for inpatient care include:

- Threats or gestures of suicide or self–harm.

- Attempts or threats to run away from home.

- Involvement in serious alcohol or drug abuse.

- The emergence of an eating disorder.

- Physical complaints or conditions that are related to emotional needs.

- Conflictual relationships among family members that have become severe.

- Hyperactivity that neither you nor your child can control.

- Fears or phobias that have become incapacitating.

- Frequent explosive fits of rage and anger.

Through the experience of inpatient treatment, children and their parents can be brought together as a unit again. The support received by a young person in a caring hospital environment can convince him of his need to examine his life in a probing manner. Similar parental support can also be found in family therapy experiences and support and educational groups for parents.

A Final Word of Encouragement

I enjoy studying the personality of the Apostle Paul because he was a man who knew hardships and lived through more than his share of traumas. Yet, he was able to write of the contentment he felt regardless of his circumstances (Phil. 4:11).

In addition to his personal sense of satisfaction, he was an encourager to others. Throughout the letters of Paul there are frequent words of encouragement to his intended readers. He was especially personal in the words which opened and closed many of his letters. Because of his endearing relationship with his readers, he was able to exercise effective leadership. At times he was harsh with his words and allowed his emotions of disappointment, disgust, and frustration to be freely viewed.

I believe Paul modeled the kind of leadership that can be exhibited in the home. In the same way that Paul used his positive rapport as a springboard for guiding others, parents can develop tools to enhance their most treasured relationships.

It is my sincere hope that as you have studied the concepts presented in this book you have learned to look inside your child. It is an exciting experience to encounter the confidence that comes from knowing that you and your child are growing together. Predictably, conflicts will still be faced, but you can expect growth to emerge from those trials.

Words of guidance written by Paul offer an appropriate closing statement. "Be wise in the way you act toward outsiders [others]; make the most of every opportunity. Let your conversation be always full of grace, seasoned with salt, so that you may know how to answer everyone" (Col. 4:5–6).

Appendix

The contents of *KidThink* may be used in a variety of ways. In addition to personal study aimed at improving relationships between parents and children, the material is useful for small group study. There are several advantages of studying a book on family relationships in a small group.

Group study may be used as a teaching forum in which a leader presents the study material to group members in an organized fashion. It is often helpful for the reader to hear an instructor explore and expand on the written material.

In addition to offering information to group members, small group activities can encourage discussion among group members. Sharing among adults can result in new perspectives and greater understanding. The support offered through small group activity gives encouragement to parents who sometimes feel alone in their family experiences. Often the knowledge that others have been through similar circumstances gives a parent the strength to adjust to his family need.

The discipline involved in small group instruction encourages parents to follow through with assignments and plans for action. Many adults report that they like feeling accountable to others to follow through with tasks even if that accountability is only implied.

For more extensive information on establishing and maintaining study groups, the reader is referred to *Handbook For Group Leaders* by Richard Price, Pat Springle, and Joe Kloba (Rapha Publishing, 1990).

Suggested Format of a Study Group

The following guidelines are offered as a potential schedule for study group activity. Of course, changes should be made to fit the specific needs of each group. Approximately 90 minutes should be allotted for each study session.

1. *Opening remarks/activities* (5–15 min.) Leaders should greet group members. If refreshments are available, they could be offered at this time. Review of the successes of the previous week's assignments could be made. In your first group session, a "get–acquainted" activity may be used during these first few minutes. A prayer asking for God's direction during the study session should be offered.

2. *Instruction* (20–30 min.) The group leader should give an overview of the material that will be discussed during the session. Each group member should have read the designated chapter. Use this instructional time to review and more completely comprehend the concepts of the chapter.

3. *Discussion* (30–40 min.) The group leader will use the discussion questions that accompany each study session as a guide to applying the concepts presented during the instructional time. Full discussion is desired, but group members should also be encouraged to reserve ample time for each question to be explored.

4. *Wrap–up* (5–15 min.) The group leader will summarize the most important points brought out in the instructional and discussion times. Assignments for the next session should be reviewed. Prayers for special family needs can be offered at this time.

Use of Study Session Material

At the end of each chapter are biblical references, discussion questions, and assignments designed for use in both individual and small group study. In all, there are 13 study sessions. One session focuses on the material in the introductory chapter. Two sessions are devoted to each of the next six chapters.

The reader is, of course, encouraged to read the chapter contents prior to using the study materials. The assignments at the end of each study session are designed to enrich your relationship with your child. They are given as a tangible way you can apply your understanding of your child.

While each child will not display every quality explored in this book, parents who have a thorough understanding of children's behavior can often prevent emotional disruption from gripping the family. A proactive approach to problem solving is always the best tactic. Parents are encouraged to study the contents of each chapter. Special focus may be given to those dynamics that are personally relevant.

The aging and wise Apostle Paul wrote his young friend, Timothy, "Do your best to present yourself to God as one approved, a workman who does not need to be ashamed and who correctly handles the word of truth" (2 Tim. 2:15). It is God's design for each of us to be well prepared for the encounters we will experience in life. Through the study of family relationships, the parent can display family leadership to his children. Our understanding of sound Christian principles of parent–child interactions can result in fulfilling changes in our families.